The Waterfalls of Wales

Rhaeadr Fawr (The Great Waterfall) in full cry at Aber, when over fifty million gallons of water fall over the cliff in twenty-four hours.

The Waterfalls of Wales

JOHN LLEWELYN JONES

ROBERT HALE · LONDON

First published in Great Britain 1986

Robert Hale Limited
Clerkenwell House
Clerkenwell Green
London EC1R 0HT

Jones, John Llewelyn
The waterfalls of Wales.
1. Waterfalls——Wales——Guide-books
2. Wales——Description and travel——
1981- ——Guide-books
I. Title
914.2′904858 GB1490

ISBN 0-7090-2584-X

Photoset in Plantin by
Kelly Typesetting Limited,
Bradford-on-Avon, Wiltshire
Printed in Great Britain by
B.A.S. Printers Limited,
Over Wallop, Hampshire
Bound by W.B.C. Bookbinders Limited

Contents

PART II

PART III

List of Illustrations

Maps

Acknowledgements

I would like to give my thanks to all who have helped with information in the preparation of this book, in particular, members of the Nature Conservancy Council at Bangor, the Forestry Commission in Wales, the North Wales National Trust, the Snowdonia National Park and the Ordnance Survey. My thanks are also due to the National Library of Wales, the Department of Geography, University of Wales, Aberystwyth, the Aberconwy Area Library, the Bristol Reference Library and the Art Library of the Victoria and Albert Museum. Any errors in the book are of course my responsibility. My thanks are due to Mrs Maureen Quantick for her valiant typing of the MS, and I also wish to acknowledge help given by Les Williams, and by Andrew Jones who provided the illustrations on pages 88, 116 and 118. The illustrations on page 6 and page 33 are reproduced by permission of the National Museum of Wales and the Frank Lane Agency. The other illustrations are by myself and my wife, who did all the processing, mapped the routes and shared the hundreds of miles of walking in the mountains and valleys of Wales.

Foreword

High on the list of the many natural delights offered to those of us who are lucky enough to live within easy reach of the high hills of Britain must be the sight and sound of falling water. I have been a waterfall fan all my life, and willingly tramp miles out of my way to see the smallest cascade marked on the Ordnance Survey map. Happily, waterfalls are liberally sprinkled over the map of my native Wales. Some, like the Swallow Falls near Bettwys-y-Coed and the falls at Devil's Bridge behind Aberystwyth, have long been major tourist attractions. Others, like the splendid Ffrwd Fawr in the wilds of Plynlimon, are visible from the roadway, but get passed by if you are not aware of their presence. Some of the best of all demand walking or even climbing to see their hidden beauties. My favourite among the secret waterfalls of Wales are the wonderful cascades at the top of the Neath Valley in South Wales. Nowhere in Britain are more falls gathered in such a small area—and every one is a beauty.

I am sure that I have still not seen all the delights of falling water that Wales has to offer. In this guide, John Llewelyn Jones has charted every important cascade in the Principality, the soothing consoling sound of cool water tumbling over stone comes to you as you turn these fascinating pages.

Wynford Vaughan-Thomas
May 1986

Introduction

The Formation of Welsh Waterfalls

Wales is rich in waterfalls. From Rhaeadr Fawr, (the Great Waterfall) near the village of Aber in the north, to the Vale of Neath in the south, as rich in the phenomena of falling water as anywhere in Europe, the waterfalls of Wales foam and thunder in full cry.

The waterfall riches of Wales originate in a combination of climatic and geological factors. Much of Wales' scenic splendour derives from mountains. The Brecon Beacons, Black Mountains, Berwyns, Arans, Cader Idris and the great Snowdonia range stretching from near Anglesey to the northern end of Cardigan Bay form an unsurpassed anthology of magnificence. Mountains always bring rain, the raw material of waterfalls, and Snowdonia, which is the most extensive area of mountain range in Wales, has the highest aggregate rainfall in the principality.

It is a simple cause-and-effect relationship. The temperature of the water-saturated air flowing in over the sea is cooled by having to rise over the mountain and also by physical contact with the cold sides of the mountains. As a result the water-vapour condenses into clouds and is eventually precipitated as rain. Parts of Snowdonia have recorded astonishing precipitation aggregates. In one year, one rain-gauge sited at 2,500 feet registered 246 inches.

A high rainfall is, however, only part of the story of Welsh Waterfalls, and the highest annual rainfall is not necessarily associated with the highest endowment of waterfalls. The average rainfall in the Vale of Neath, for example, varies from sixty to ninety inches a year, far less than Snowdonia or Plynlimon, but the waterfall and gorge splendour of the Vale is unsurpassed. One has to seek the basic causes elsewhere, particularly in the geological factors.

Waterfalls are never found where a river flows for the whole of its life over a homogenous hard rock formation, free from fractures and planes of weakness. Over such a uniform geological bed, a river would eventually form a gentle slope with just enough gradient to maintain flow, a state which geologists refer to as an 'ideal base line'. Nature's ideal in all her affairs is the achievement of equilibrium, and in the case of the river bed, equilibrium consists of a smooth, very slightly inclined profile. But this achievement of the 'ideal base line' is very rare, and in the real world a river bed in which the ups and downs have been largely eliminated is described as a ' graded bed'.

The first major cause of waterfalls is the mingling of different rock strata, because soft and hard rocks differ markedly in their resistance to running water. Where hard

4 *In the Vale of Neath many waterfalls are produced when the water falls over ledges cut by the rivers in the Millstone grit. These Falls are on the Nedd Fechan (Little Neath).*

Hard rocks are often affected by 'joints'—partings or fractures—and when the soft rock underneath is eaten away by waterfall splash, the hard rock falls away in symmetrical boulders, as here at the Melincourt Falls.

and soft deposits mingle in the river bed, there will be no graded bed, no evenness of course. The bed will consist of alternating stretches of gentle slopes as the river flows over hard, erosion-resistance rock, with intervening steep drops where the soft rock has been eaten away faster by the eroding river. For example, a river flowing over hard, quartz-rich sandstone with its grains cemented together by silica will make little impression on the rock, but if the sandstone occurs in a conjunction of strata which includes a fissile shale, to which the river gains access, the river will 'eat away' the

Scŵd Gwladys encased in ice. The icicles under the cornice of sandstone illustrate how the water seeps through the joints and bedding planes of the hard rock.

shale so that the sandstone rocks will stand out and become 'falls-makers', over which the river has to tumble in the form of cascades and waterfalls.

But waterfalls do also occur in some areas of homogeneous hard rock, e.g. sandstone and conglomerate, because, although these may be highly resistant to river erosion and to the other erosion agents, they are sometimes affected by 'joints' (fractures) or 'planes of weakness', so that they tend to break away in large, symmetrical boulders, producing rocky ledges over which the river falls in the form of cascades and waterfalls. The occurrence of some Welsh waterfalls is also associated with 'geological faults' where pressures in the earth's crust cause permanent dislocation and displacement in the strata, so that rocks may be tilted, folded, lifted or fractured, with cracks which may run for tens of miles. The erosive action of running water can then cut more deeply into the soft rocks exposed in the fault zone, and this leads to waterfalls. Some Welsh waterfalls have also been formed at sites where 'sills' or 'dykes' of super-hard igneous rocks—rock formed from the cooling and solidification of molten rock material—have been intruded into the softer, sedimentary strata (page 191).

A number of Welsh waterfalls are associated with river takeovers in which sister rivers or tributaries 'capture' the waters of other rivers and greatly increase their own erosive power. This may occur when a river which has a common source with other rivers, e.g. on the slopes of the same hills or mountains, because of subsequent differences of bedrock and inequalities in slopes and gradients, cuts across the course of a sister stream, beheads it and captures its water (river 'piracy').

A waterfall may also be created at a 'knickpoint'. A 'knickpoint' is associated with a change in the gradient of a stream bed, due to a relative rise of the land *vis-à-vis* sea-level, and occurs where the old and the new exponential long profiles meet.

The other major agent of Welsh waterfall-making is a legacy from the Ice Age. In the valleys along the steep faces of the mountains, great glaciers accumulated, sending their all-conquering tongues of ice in all directions. The grit and rock debris embedded in the base of the glaciers as they moved with inexorable slowness down the valleys enabled them to act like giant excavators along the valley floor. The bigger and deeper the original valley and the mightier the glacier, the more deeply the valley was gouged and ground down. As a consequence, many of the tributary subsidiary valleys which were affected by smaller glaciers and were less deeply excavated were left 'hanging' high above the main valley, and the rivers from these 'hanging valleys' had to fall into the main drainage areas in the form of waterfalls. Though the occurrence of waterfalls in any part of Wales may be associated with both hanging valleys and differential erosion, it is broadly true that differential erosion of soft and hard rock along the river bed is more typically a waterfall cause in South Wales, and the occurrence of hanging valley waterfalls is more typical in the north where the mountains are higher, the slopes steeper and the original valleys deeper.

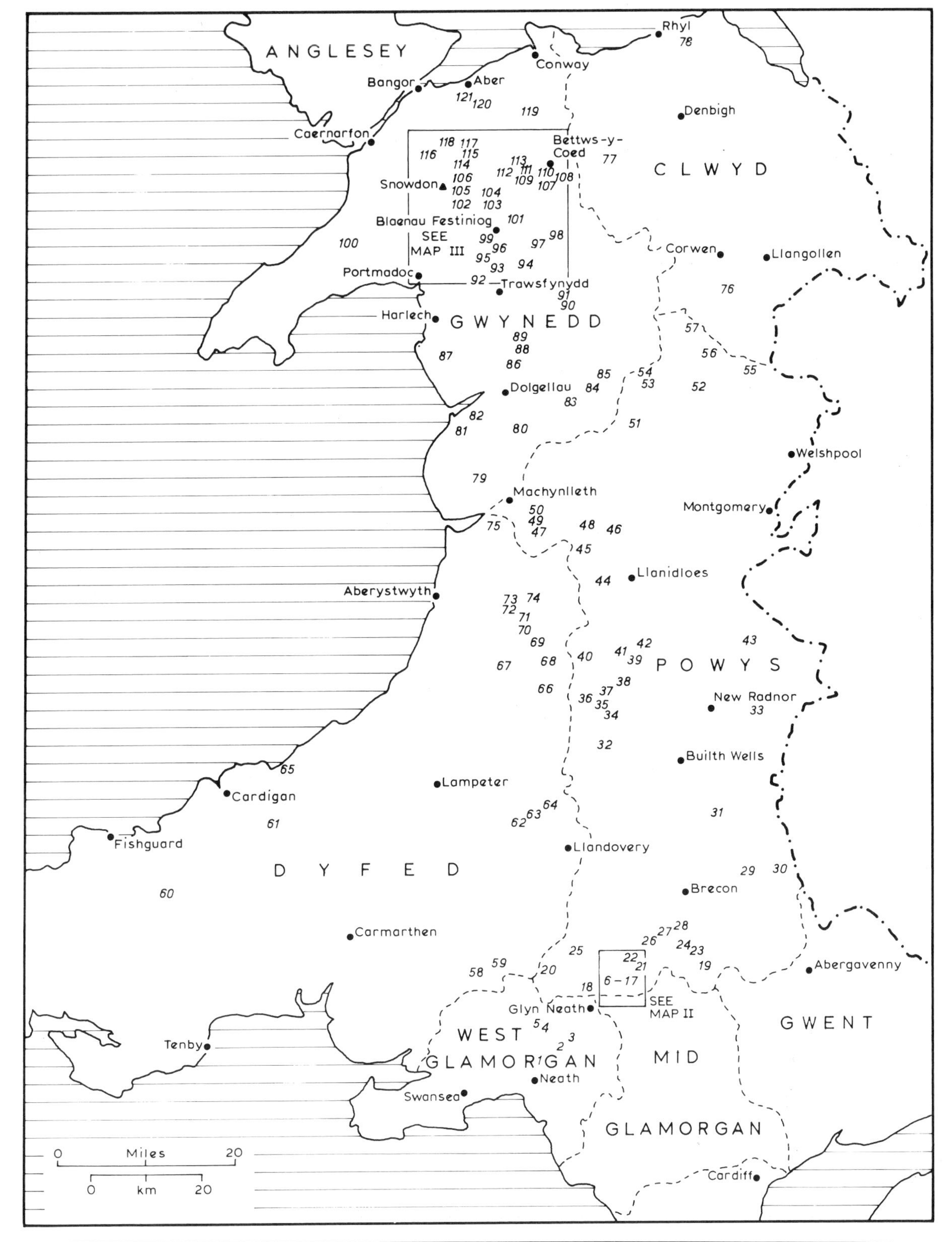

MAP I: *Distribution and location of waterfalls in Wales.*

The beginning of the great glacial rock step at Nant Ffrancon down which the rivers Ogwen and Idwal fall. In the background the mist-swathed three-pointed summit of 'Tryfan'.

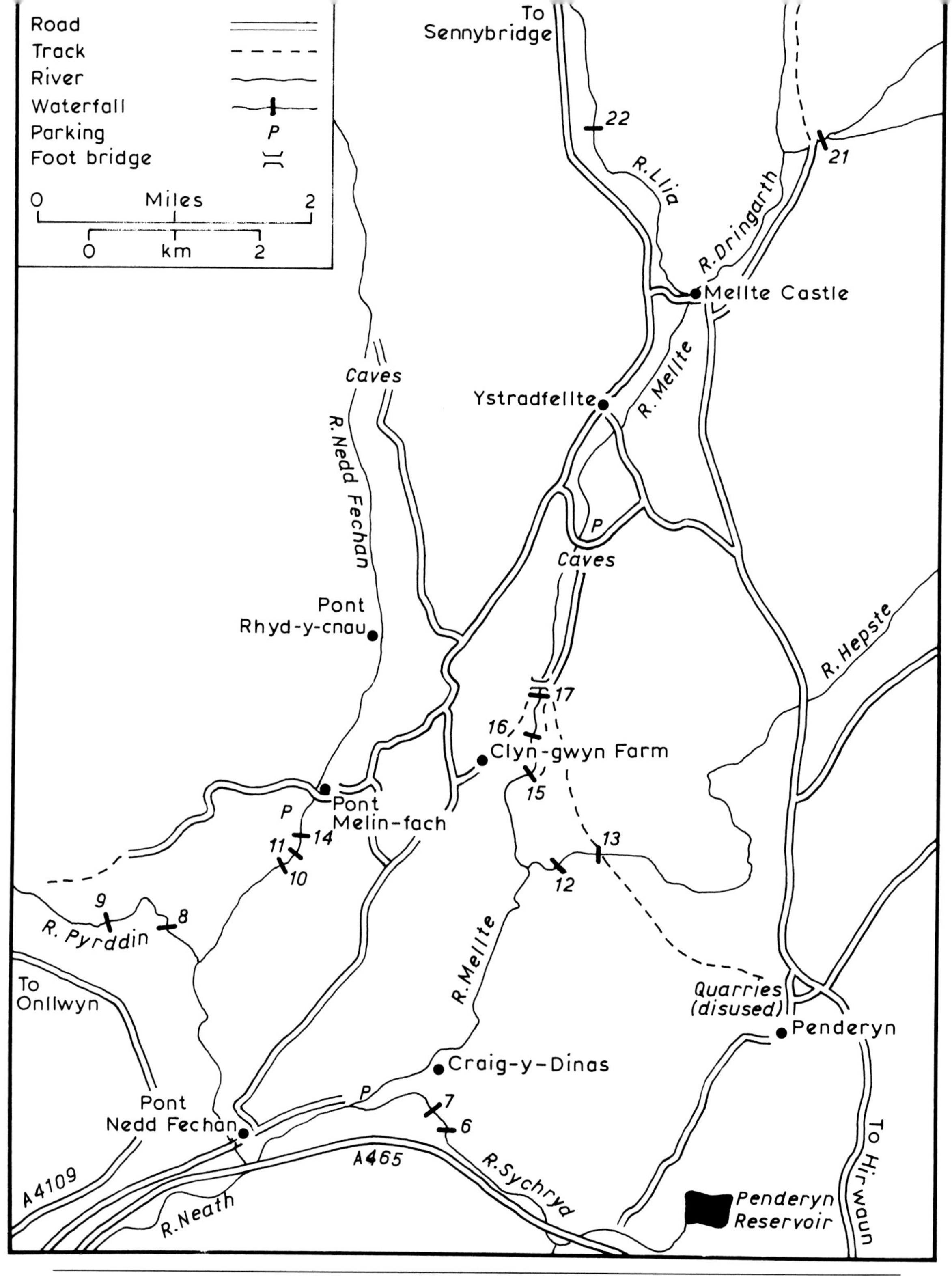

MAP II: *Distribution and location of waterfalls in the Vale of Neath.*

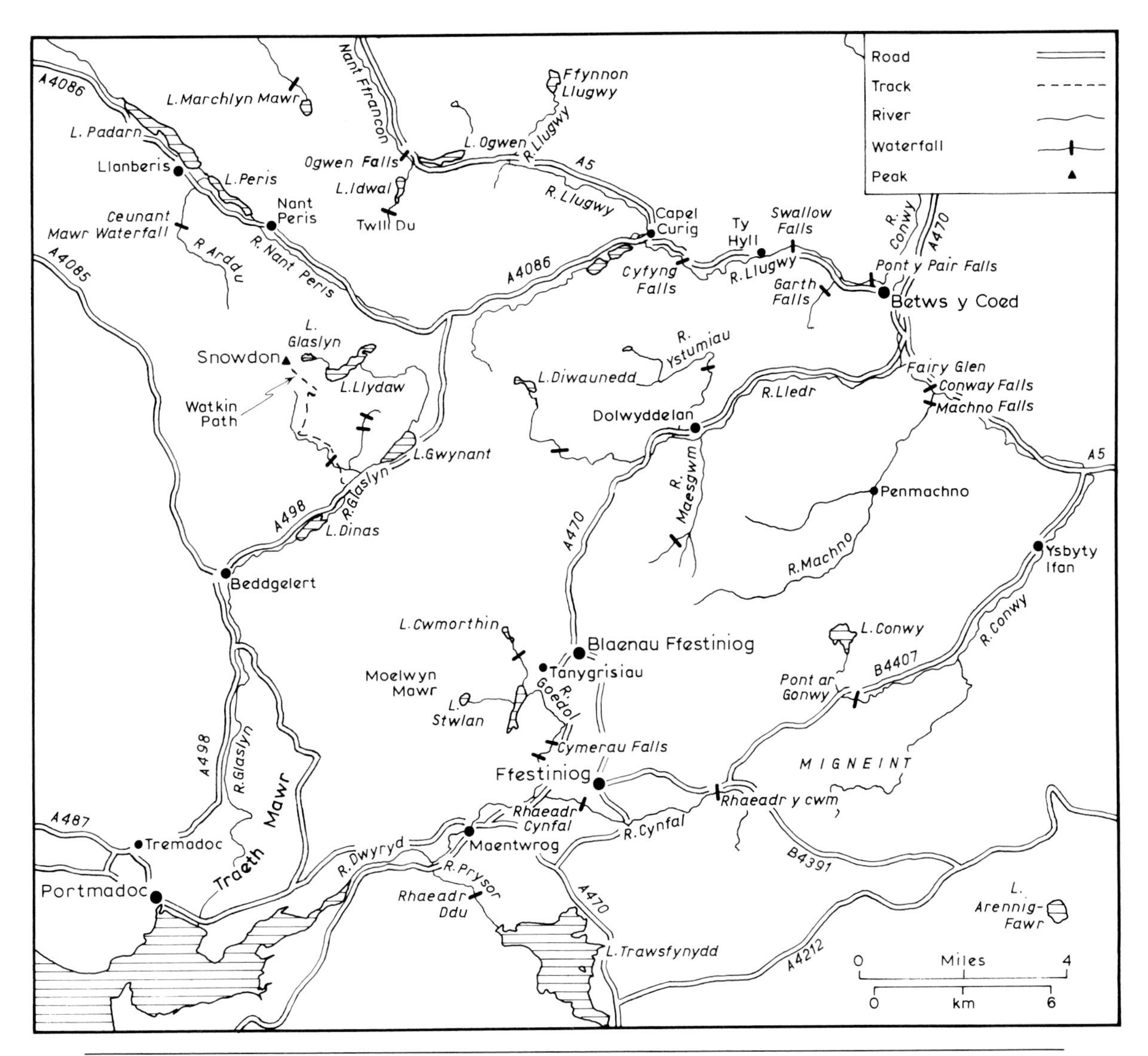

MAP III: Distribution and location of waterfalls in Snowdonia.

The Waterfall Regions of Wales

Nowhere in Wales are waterfalls due to the differential erosion of hard and soft rocks found in greater variety than in the Vale of Neath in South Wales, where there are twelve major waterfalls to regale the searcher. The Vale, often in Wales described as 'the waterfall country', is in the new collective of Powys and comprises a series of steep-sided, interlinked, wooded glens and gorges traversed by six rivers, the Mellte, Hepste, Pyrddin, Nedd Fechan (Little Neath), Sychryd and Neath. There is a gladitorial contest of these waters for riverine supremacy until the River Neath eventually takes over all her companions and winds to the sea like a swollen boa-constrictor.

The vale is well served by approach roads, even if they are mostly minor in the end phases: from Neath to the village of Pont Nedd Fechan via Glyn Neath, from Merthyr Tydfil via the A465 road through Hirwaun and across the moors to Penderyn village, and from Brecon along the A470 via Storey Arms, now an outdoor leisure centre. Of the five main rivers, the Nedd Fechan, the Mellte and the Hepste rise on the southern slopes of Fforest Fawr, near Fan Nedd and Fan Gyhirych at heights between 1,500 and 2,000 feet. (The Fanau or Vans are the hills which run east over Fforest Fawr to the Brecon Beacons and west into the Black Mountain). The Pyrddin rises on lower ground further south, and the Sychryd on the northern slopes of the Craig-y-Llyn escarpment with its glacial cwms.

From their red and purple Old Red Sandstone cradles on the smooth-topped Vans, the Nedd Fechan, the Mellte (the latter formed at a delightful confluence point of the rivers Llia and Dringarth) and the Hepste flow southwards through the mixed geological formations of the 'waterfall country' of the Vale. While passing through the hard, erosion-resistant Old Red Sandstone, the rivers flow in shallow troughs of rock which they have cut on their way into the belt of Upper Carboniferous rocks. When they enter the Carboniferous belt they flow through a region formed of rocks of varying degrees of hardness and resistance to river erosion. The upper layer in the Carboniferous rock is usually Millstone Grit (a form of sandstone in which the grains are angular rather than rounded and so named because of the extreme hardness which made it suitable for fashioning millstones) surmounting bands of softer, fossiliferous shale, interbedded with limestone. It is here that the waterfalls really begin, for while the Millstone Grit and other associate hard conglomerates are themselves resistant to river erosion they belong to the basically 'unstable' strata mentioned earlier which are

In perspective the Vale of Neath appears as a belt of trees surrounded by meadows and high moors and gives no hint of the waterfall tumult within.

affected by 'joints' and 'bedding planes', resulting in the production of cracks or fractures in the rock (lateral or vertical). These fractures which are enlarged by ice, or other weathering factors give the river flowing across them access to the lower, softer shales, which they then begin to eat away, so that progressively the harder, erosion-resistant rocks are deprived of their support from below and eventually fall away at their joints. Waterfalls ensue.

The production of waterfalls in this mixed Millstone Grit area of the Vale has also been fostered and hastened by the increasing velocity flow of the rivers as they approach the Carboniferous limestone belt. This increased rate of flow and the resultant increase in down-cutting power are due to the fact that the main Neath Valley, which they are approaching and into which they drain, was more heavily deepened by a master glacier between Glyn Neath and Neath. This increased gradient greatly increases the erosive power of the rivers—it is estimated that, when the velocity of a river is doubled, its erosive power can be increased by a factor of up to sixty times—as they roar through their deep, narrow gorges to eventual confluence with the Neath. This same deepening of the Neath Valley by glacier action has also resulted in some of the rivers outside the Vale having to descend from hanging valleys and has led to the formation of some fine hanging valley waterfalls such as the Melincourt Falls (page 47). As well as their association with individual fractures, joints and bedding planes in the hard rock, waterfalls in the Vale are also associated with geological 'faults' due to permanent dislocation of the continuity of the strata.

Paradoxically, these same fractures and faults in the Millstone Grits which have produced such a wealth of waterfalls also cause the rivers to disappear completely for longer or shorter periods at some stages in their lives. This is because the limestones to which these fractures have given access are to some degree soluble in acid-carrying rainwater. When this acid rain percolates from above into the joints and fissures of the well-jointed limestone, these fissures are eventually enlarged into channels, and underground caverns may be formed capable of carrying the whole river which, up above, then becomes a dry bed. Nedd Fechan, Hepste, Mellte and Sychryd all disappear underground at some stage when they pass from the hard sandstone of their adolescence to the Carboniferous limestone of their maturity.

But the most important disappearance is that of the Mellte, which disappears into the limestone cave system of Porth yr Ogof (Portal of the Cave), at a point just over half a mile due south of the village of Ystradfellte. (The site of the cave is now served by a Forestry Commission car-park, from which visitors can also walk to the two upper Mellte waterfalls.) One enters through a fifty-foot-wide entrance, for the cave is roofed over with a massive lintel of limestone rock. The river disappears underground for 972 feet before re-emerging into daylight through a deep cleft in the rock, to resume its turbulent course to the first waterfall, Scŵd Clungwyn (page 63), half a mile downstream. Caves such as Porth yr Ogof provide a key to the limestone gorges of the Vale. The river, flowing and carving out its passage underground, was originally roofed over by such a stratum of rock. Eventually this began to collapse at the river's point of ingress and then continued to collapse progressively along the underground course of the river, to form the present limestone gorges.

A tantalizing feature of the Vale 'waterfall country' which has excited rueful comment over the years is the extent to which it conceals its unique anthology of treasures. The rivers flowing in their deep, steep gorges are literally invisible from any distance, except for short periods in the north. Seen as a perspective, there is no hint from any outside vantage-point of the tumult of waters along the mixed geological strata and ravines, the brief honeymooning of their confluences, their descents into limestone netherworlds. All one sees is a long, narrow belt of woodland surrounded by moorland and meadows. Until recently, when the Neath local authorities in partnership with the Manpower Services Commission eased and marked out the approaches, it was only too easy to set out for Scŵd yr Eira, for example (page 53) from the village of Penderyn, to walk across the moorland approach and to return to one's starting-point having completely failed to find the only safe way down to the falls. The descent is in fact down the gully which marks the occurrence of the 'fault' where the Scŵd yr Eira waterfall originated, and it is signalled by the presence of two huge boulders with splashes of pink paint, on the edge of the escarpment. These are 'glacial erratics', deposited here by the retreating, melting glaciers, and they mark the place where it is safe and possible to descend to the waterfall, though even here the roar of the falls is virtually indistinguishable from the sound of the river in full flow. An early explorer, painter and writer, William Weston Young, who published a charming little book in 1835 on the beauties of the Vale which was illustrated with fourteen hand-coloured, ink and captioned etchings and was entitled *Guide to the Beauties of Glyn Neath*) was moved to express in rueful verse his failures to find Scŵd yr Eira:

> Oft have I gained this mountainside
> And on the world looked down and scanned
> The many devious ways I've tried
> To reach the spot where now I stand.

It is a frustration which has been experienced by most of us sometime, seeking the dividends which this superstar has to offer its admirers.

Scŵd yr Eira is a relatively small waterfall compared, for example, with Rhaeadr Fawr (the Great Waterfall) of Aber, but it is undeniably one of the most interesting (page 189) in Wales. Apart from its grace, it is the geomorphic British miniature of the Niagara Falls. Like its gigantic analogue of the New World, Scŵd yr Eira is what the geologists describe as a 'waterfall in a state of recession'. It had its origins in a rock fault which crosses the Hepste in the form of a gully on the right-hand bank of the river about fifty yards below the present site of the waterfall. This fault in the Millstone Grit gave the river access to the middle band of softer shale, and the splash of the water landing on the hard grit below the shale ate into the softer band between the top and bottom layers of the grit so that as the process continued, the top overhang of rock, progressively undermined from below, eventually fell away. In this way the precipice over which the river fell was progressively restored to a more or less perpendicular profile, and the waterfall had receded a few feet upstream. (The hard rock fronting Scŵd yr Eira has also been carved by the falling water into steps of almost man-made symmetry.)

It is difficult to assess the length of time it has taken for Scŵd yr Eira to recede upstream from the original fault to its present position. The only carefully documented record for the recession of a waterfall is in the case of the Niagara river. Instrumental surveys covering nearly 150 years, taken in conjunction with visual observations (the first made as long ago as 1658), show that the giant waterfall is retreating upstream at an average rate of over three feet per year. As the falls are about twelve thousand years old, this means it has receded upstream over 7½ miles since the last Ice Age. The mechanism of recession, the removal of the soft shale by the splash of the falls and the breakaway of the top rock overhang, is identical with that occurring with Scŵd yr Eira except that the top hard strata at Niagara are composed of hard Silurian limestone, whereas at Scŵd yr Eira the Hepste river flows over a hard sandstone.

While differential erosion accounts for much of the waterfall grandeur of the Vale of Neath, glaciation in the surrounding area has also played a role. In particular, the glacier from the Brecon Beacons, which eroded and deepened the lower Neath valley, caused the Nedd Fechan and the Mellte in turn to increase their own velocity of flow and the rate of their down-cutting, which hastened the formation of other waterfalls. The glacier which penetrated the Neath and other valleys accumulated initially along the sandstone 'table-top' heights and slopes of the Brecon Beacons and other ranges, which sent forth great tongues of ice down the valleys, in all directions, even as far as the Bristol Channel. In the Brecon Beacons the accumulating ice and snow were deeper and longer-lasting along the steep north-facing slopes and pre-glacial hollows. Below the giant precipice of Pen y Fan the huge, long-lasting glacier ground off the lateral spurs of rock, steepened the mountain slopes and deepened the pre-glacial hollow into a deep basin at the foot of the mountain wall. Then the melting glacier deposited large mounds of rock and other debris, now grassed over as large moraines (hummocks) behind which the present mountain tarn of Llyn Cwm Llwch formed. This glacial corrie lake is now the source of Nant Cwm Llwch which with its tributary streamlets produces the major water spectacular of the Beacons as they fall down a series of glacial steps which have also been accentuated by differential erosion and which makes the approach to Pen y Fan and Corn Du one of the finest mountain walks in South Wales (page 79). These corrie lakes impounded behind glacial moraines are among the best-known features of the Brecon Beacons National Park and include Llyn y Fan Fach and Llyn y Fan Fawr (page 75) in the Black Mountain.

As one moves north-ward from the Vale and the Beacons, the principal waterfall areas of mid-Wales are the Vale of Rheidol, particularly the area of the Devil's Bridge, and the Plynlimon range of hills. The waterfalls of the Devil's Bridge ravine provide the most spectacular example in the whole of Britain of the effect of river capture (page 117-19). The great depth of the Rheidol gorge is due to the fact that the original course of the Upper Rheidol/Teifi was diverted by the headward erosion of the Ystwyth along the 'Ystwyth Fault' and then by the Lower Rheidol, through a series of 'captures'. This enormously increased the down-cutting power of the Rheidol, with the result that the River Mynach entering the ravine has to fall 400 feet to join the River Rheidol flowing below. Generations of travellers have written with awe and admiration of the waterfalls of this part of mid-Wales which at one time formed part of the famous 'Hafod' estate (page 113).

Another main waterfall area of mid-Wales is the Plynlimon range which in places rises to almost 2,500 feet and is the source of five rivers, including the tempestuous Rheidol itself. The highest Plynlimon waterfalls are those which fall off the northern edge of the escarpment. The River Twymyn, which drops into an awesome gorge near the old mining village of Dyliffe (page 97), provides a particularly fine example of a waterfall associated with river capture.

Proceeding north, one enters the great expanse of the Snowdonia National Park, which covers 845 square miles stretching from Cader Idris in the south to Aber in the north and from Llanberis in the west to Bala in the east. The Park territory is richly endowed with waterfalls associated with a variety of geological factors, but there are some particularly dramatic examples of the 'hanging valley' waterfalls, of which Nant Ffrancon furnishes a memorable instance. Nant Ffrancon runs from Llyn Ogwen on the A5 to the little town of Bethesda, and everywhere the evidence of glaciation is visible.

It is astonishing that as recently as the middle of the last century belief in a British Ice Age was still no part of the scientific credo, so that even the great Darwin (who visited Snowdonia's Cwm Idwal (page 183) in 1851 with a colleague, Professor Sedgewick, to search for fossils and to study the geology of the region) failed to appreciate the clamant evidence of the Ice Age literally under his nose. Darwin was subsequently to refer to his astonishing myopia in a rueful confession that, 'We spent many hours in Cwm Idwal examining all the rocks with extreme care as Sedgewick is anxious to find fossils in them but neither of us saw the phenomena all around us. We did not notice the plainly scarred rocks, the perched boulders, the lateral and terminal moraines. Yet these phenomena are so conspicuous that a house burned down did not tell its story more plainly than did this valley . . . ' Professor Sedgewick, however, stayed unconvinced and refused to accept that Britain had ever had an Ice Age, remaining an 'unbeliever' to the end of his life.

Nant Ffrancon was occupied by one of Snowdonia's most massive glaciers, when the range must have looked something like the Arctic today, with the incessant snow which built up above the snowline being continuously compressed, until the vast weight of the compressing ice began to force it to bulge outwards and, obedient to the

force of gravity, it began to move. The ice colossus of Nant Ffrancon, with boulders embedded in its base and fed with supplementary streams of ice from the Glyders and the Carneddau which tower over the sides of the valley, moved relentlessly and inexorably down the existing valley, gouging and deepening the valley floor into the characteristic U-shape, the 'armchair hollow' of the Snowdonia cwm (corrie), shearing off the lateral spurs of rock, deepening and straightening and bevelling the sides, all the way from the foot of Pen yr Ole Wen (Peak of the White Light) to the present town of Bethesda.

At the head of this glaciated valley, Nant Ffrancon provides a fine example of a glacier-associated waterfall, in the form of Rhaeadr Ogwen (page 181). The waterfall should perhaps be more appropriately called the Ogwen and Idwal falls for the water draining from Llyn Ogwen in the form of the River Ogwen and from Cwm Idwal in the river of that name join together in their gigantic tumble down the 'glacial rock step' of over 200 feet into the valley below. The fangs and outcrops of hard rock and the boulders among and over which the marrying white waters of the two rivers leap and seethe bear remarkable evidence of the passage of the ice, for on the upstream side the rocks have been gently sloped and smoothed by the glacier's passage, while on the downstream side they have been roughened and steepened by the glacier. Such individual rocks or boulders which have been subjected to this sort of glacial action are given the name '*roches moutonnées*', a description first applied by a French geologist of the eighteenth century who thought they resembled the sheepskin wigs ('*moutonnées*') in vogue at the time! In all respects, Nant Ffrancon, with its hanging cwms and waterfalls, is a dramatic example of an Ice Age valley and has been used as a 'model' to depict how the glaciated valley probably looked during the Ice Age. The Nant Ffrancon model can be seen in the Museum of Geology at South Kensington, where the master glacier can be seen coming out of Cwm Idwal, with smaller glaciers in the tributary valleys around.

The stream Nant Cwm Llwch has its source in the sombre waters of Llyn Cwm Llwch, which lies under the frown of Pen y Fan (Top of the Mountain, 2,906 feet) and provides an example of a valley-headed lake impounded by a crescent-shaped Ice Age moraine.

The Lure of Waterfalls

However they are formed, waterfalls are special features of Welsh scenery. On the darkest day they show and shine from afar, call and beckon with giant voices as they fall through the air. Apart from their cousins, the river torrents, they are the sole vocal features in the landscape. The white water of the falls signals the place, the location; the voice uniquely proclaims that one of Nature's spectacular unions is taking place, the white marriage of water and gravity.

In some ways the appeal of Welsh waterfalls is the antithesis of that of Welsh lakes, with which the cwms of Wales are plentifully endowed. Theirs are the beautiful waters of silence. Welsh mountain lakes are almost always brooding and dark, spreading their lacustrine melancholy over the landscape (except when they hold white clouds or when the sky is blue enough to brush a faint cerulean on their sombre silk), whereas waterfalls are never-failingly white, even on dark days. This is especially true of those falls that are formed with clean mountain water which has been flowing over hard rock, because the perfectly pure, clear droplets reflect back equally all the different wavelengths of light throughout the spectrum. The purer the water, the whiter the falls.

Though some of them may be dauntingly difficult to find, it is the nature of waterfalls to be ebullient self-advertisers of their position as the action highlights of the river, and knowledge of their presence up or down stream provides a lure which always gives an expedition the quality of a treasure-hunt. One walks along the river bank where this is possible (though often it is a question of keeping as close to the shouting water as the steepness and tanglewood of screes will allow), peering through the trees for tell-tale glimpses of white water, listening for the summons of the falls, often indistinguishable from the river, until finally, through the shrouding green canopy of summer or the turning leaves of autumn or the skeleton sticks and dark trunks of winter (which more than any other season reveals all), one hears the roar and catches a glimpse of the beckoning water of the falls. Most of the remote Welsh waterfalls are sited in solitude, where human encounters are rare, and, in the really deep ravines, have to be admired from the top of the gorge or escarpment. But whether one comes face to face with the fulfilment of the search or not, the excitement of discovery is always there.

Another of the attractions of Welsh waterfalls is their individuality. Within the shared fact of being water phenomena, they are as different as human beings. While the position of the waterfall can be easily explained—even forecast—by the presence of hard or soft formations or a massive rock outcrop, the shape and form of the waterfall, its 'personality', is the product of a permutation of factors: the type of rock, the presence and position of fractures, faults, bedding planes, arch-like (anticlinal) lifts or troughlike (synclinal) dips, the average volume and flow of water, the effect of weathering on the valley sides. These factors produce dramatically different results so that even waterfalls in close proximity on the same river, can be totally distinctive. At Scŵd yr Eira (page 53), for example, the River Hepste falls in a graceful, aqueous arch over the precipice of fall, while a hundred yards away its sister falls, the Lower Cilhepste (page 57) rushes like a speeding locomotive down its steep-sided sandstone gorge. Scŵd Gwladys (page 49) and Scŵd Einion Gam (page 51) on the same river are so completely unlike as hardly to belong to the same generic category.

In one sense, the waterfall is the chameleon of landscape. It can change in a matter of days from the highlight of a river in spate, thundering through the valleys and mountains surrounds, to the soft-spoken apotheosis of the river at peace, as it flows with gentle sparseness through a thirsting landscape. Within a short period, the same falls—Rhaeadr Fawr (page 189)—can present two totally different 'faces', the one dramatic and speech-eclipsing after heavy rain, the other falling down its granite cliffs in drought, with enchanting gentleness.

But whatever their moods, waterfalls are sociable creatures. They may be avalanching and roaring through the air, and yet one can be at peace close by, to rest or picnic or just stand and admire. The only moving water phenomenon which broadcasts a message comparable to the waterfall in full cry is the sea in storm, combers hounded into foaming giants by the gale. But one cannot enjoy in comfort the spectacle of the stormy sea. One's instinct always is to 'get out of the wind'.

Not surprisingly perhaps, the waterfall, with its refreshing ambience of water-cooled air, is claimed by one school of thought to possess positive health-giving qualities. The theory is that 'waterfall air' is refreshing and invigorating because of the negatively charged molecules or 'negative ions' which are produced by the pluvial might of the falls breaking up the molecules of air. ('Air ionisation' is the general term used to describe the production of air molecules which carry a minute positive or negative charge of electricity.) Most air molecules, it seems, do not carry any electrical charge at all, and even in country air the number so charged is only about one in 500 million million. The health properties are supposedly contained only in those carrying a negative charge, and there are more of these health-giving negative ions in the air ambience of the waterfall than in other natural sources, e.g. ultra-violet rays from the sun, cosmic rays and lightning. The claim that much of the lassitude of modern living is due to the negative depletion of polluted air may or may not be valid. But there is no doubt of the power of the waterfall in full voice—which, despite the transiency of its decibelic might, sounds as though it will go on forever—to thin out the queue of anxious moments, massage the mind with its roaring peace.

Part of the lure of Welsh waterfalls is in the trees and plants with which they are associated. If one had to nominate a tree which is *par excellence* the 'waterfall tree', the choice would unhesitatingly be the rowan or mountain ash. For the mountain waterfall hunter, the rowan is the true sylvan adornment of the high falls for it grows at greater altitudes than any other tree and may be encountered up to 3,000 feet. In the immediate environs of high waterfalls it finds a colonizable habitat, for rocky mountain falls are invariably associated with the light soil which the rowan favours, never the clays and soft limestones which it abhors. The ability of the reddish-brown rowan seed to germinate, and of the subsequent seedlings to find anchorage and make growth in the meagre soil of rocky ledges and crannies in the bleakest positions, is incredible. One cannot but be moved when one is near the limit of one's own physical endurance after a long mountain scramble or ascent to find a little rowan grimly hanging on to its precarious habitat.

By many mountain waterfalls the rowan hangs its profusion of scarlet berries almost into the white water. On the treeless heights of the Brecon Beacons in the approach to Pen y Fan and Corn Du (the highest points) a group of rowans crowd round the waterfall of Nant Cwm Llwch, seeming to grow literally out of the rock, driven to a crouching survival stance by the wind. Near the top of the great wall of rock with which the Glyder Fawr mountain descends into Cwm Idwal, I have watched for years one little rowan that seems to grow no bigger with the passage of time but is always there, despite the massed onslaught of the elements, flaunting its unconquerable capacity to survive.

Rowans can, of course, grow into magnificent trees where the conditions are more favourable. The finest assemblage of scarlet branches I have ever seen is to be found below Pistyll Rhaeadr, the highest of the Welsh waterfalls. Crowded out from the immediate environs of the falls by the larches, beech and oak trees planted in the nineteenth century by Sir Watcyn Williams Wynne, who owned the gorge, the rowans have established themselves in magnificent profusion among the slate rocks of a nearby slope on the Berwyn foothills. Apart from the 240-foot waterfall, the rowans alone are worth a visit in their own right.

But waterfalls also have their own particular plants, especially where the spray from the waterfall is off base rocks which provide a flow of minerals and other nutrients. Ferns in particular grace the waterfall habitat, the filmy fern, royal fern, hay-scented mountain buckler fern and, on northfacing cliffs near waterfalls, the rare Tunbridge filmy fern and the Wilson fern. Many other uncommon plants are characteristically found near waterfalls, and of course a host of mosses and liverworts. Providing colour near the waterfalls, especially when base-rich water falls from limestone, are water avens, valerians, golden saxifrage, (the much less common) starry saxifrage, yellow archangel, tutsan, common butterwort and small-leaved limes, as well as the gold and purple of flowering gorse and heather.

The waterfall search described in this book takes us into some of the loneliest and wildest parts of Wales. On many of these journeys of quest we shall seem to be the only humans in the world. But from time to time there are rewarding encounters on the way. We accept as normal the mountain-booted, haversacked figures for whom seeking the joys of the countryside is a way of life. But I recall also, with the utmost pleasure, a party of boisterous lads aged from nine to twelve years from a home for children with discipline and behavioural problems, on holiday near Brecon. Their two young guardians had brought them on a visit to the valley of the Mellte where the drama of the waterfalls, the speed of the tumultuous rivers, wading in bare feet along the top of Scŵd Isaf Clungwyn to cross to the other bank, the goat-jump challenge of mid-stream rocks, the muscle-testing search for the elusive Scŵd y Pannwr, the third waterfall, provided them with all the challenge needed to soak up their exhibitionism and derring-do. They loved it.

The environs of waterfalls are particularly rich in ferns, many of them rare, liverworts and mosses, and many colourful flowers. (Pistyll y Llyn.)

Then there was the lady who had had her arthritic hip joint replaced but was still determined to lead her family in the giddy search for Scŵd yr Eira, and the elderly angina sufferer walking slowly on his wife's arm in the waterfall glen of Pwll-y-Wrach (page 85) because he wanted to photograph a certain bog orchid on his way. Most memorable of all perhaps was returning from Pistyll y Llyn (page 99) when a car drew up with the familiar enquiry: 'Is this the way to the waterfall?' I met the driver of the car the following day at the Furnace Falls near Eglwysfach and voiced a polite hope that they had found the waterfall. 'Yes, indeed', was the reply. 'We got at least half way there, the best they had ever done.' Then I saw that 'they' were a happy pair of beautiful midgets, a husband and wife, whose little legs had so bravely conquered half the rough track of Pistyll y Llyn to enjoy the cataract in boisterous mood after twenty-four hours of rain.

There was also the carpenter and his wife from Taunton in Somerset who said that they used waterfalls as lodestars when planning the day's expedition, because the word 'waterfalls' on the map almost invariably signified areas of outstanding beauty so that scouring the Welsh Ordnance Maps to find the evocative word was in their experience a virtually foolproof system of ensuring an exciting walk with a glittering target.

The searcher for waterfalls in lonely, rough country should be well shod and clad and take a compass.

Poets and Painters of Welsh Waterfalls

Welsh waterfall country has attracted the attention of many poets and artists down the centuries. One of the earliest to celebrate the Vale of Neath waterfall rivers was the Elizabethan poet Michael Drayton, in his poetic narrative published in 1622, written in vigorous twelve-syllabled verse and bearing what surely must be the longest title of any topographical book, *Polyolbion—a Chorographical Description of All the Tracts, Rivers, Mountains, Forests and Other Parts of Great Britain*. It is a *tour de force* packed with geological, historical and regional detail of surprising accuracy. The style is typified in the opening description of the waterfall rivers of the Vale when the poet describes

> . . . where nimble Nedd
> To all her neighbouring nymphs for her rare beauty known
> Beside her double head to keep her stream that hath
> Her handmaids Melta, sweet clear Hepsay and Tringarth
> From Brecon forth doth break . . .

Another poet, a Welshman who lived near the Vale of Neath and was more or less a Drayton contemporary, wrote a poem about a Welsh waterfall which is among his most memorable. Henry Vaughan was born at Llansantffraid, a little village in the shadow of the Brecon Beacons. He called himself 'the Silurist' after the Welsh tribe of the Silures in south-east Wales who for a long period stubbornly resisted conquest by the Romans. Vaughan returned to his birthplace to practise medicine and write his poems after a period of persecution for supporting the Royalist cause. Known as 'the Swan of Usk', he was a member of the 'metaphysical' school of English poetry, for whom the natural world was often the vehicle of highly concentrated 'conceits' used to convey religious truths. Vaughan's poem about a waterfall is one of the best of his 'Nature poems', but the principal use of the waterfall is as a religious symbol. The poet describes how the river seems to hang back as it approaches the precipice and calls out as though in fear:

> With what deep mirrors through time's silent stealth,
> Doth thy transparent, cool and watery wealth,
> Here flowing fall
> And climbe and call
> As if his liquid loose retinue stood
> Lingring, and were of this steep place afraid.

But he draws comfort because, after its descent into the plunge pool, the river does not in fact meet its end but acquires renewed strength. He describes how he sees it

Quickened by the deep and rocky grave
Rise to a longer course more bright and brave.

So in like fashion we can draw comfort that death is not to be feared because it is the beginning of the new, true life.

Wordsworth too had a particular love for rivers and waterfalls and like many of his contemporaries, Coleridge, Southey, Shelley, de Quincey, Hazlitt and Peacock, travelled in Wales to enjoy its mountains and glens, its castles and romantic ruins and particularly its waterfalls. He was greatly moved by the power of the Mynach Waterfall of the Devil's Bridge gorge, near Aberystwyth (page 117). He visited the area after heavy rain and also, it should be remembered, at a time before the tempestuous Rheidol had been deflowered of some of its might by the hydro-electric schemes of the present century.

Wordsworth's sonnet 'To the Torrent at the Devil's Bridge in North Wales' was published in 1827. The opening lines which describe his awe as he watched the Mynach falling 400 feet into the Rheidol below, are followed by characteristic imagery:

How art thou named? In search of what strange land
From what huge height descending? Can such force
Of waters issue from a British source;
Or hath not Pindus fed thee where the band
Of patriots scoop their freedom out with hand
Desperate as thine?

Of the many famous nineteenth century writers to visit Wales, none fell in love more deeply with its waterfalls than a contemporary of Wordsworth's, Thomas Love Peacock, often anthologized as though he were merely the poet of tribal Welsh rapine, in his 'War Song of Dinas Fawr.' A close friend of Shelley, a tireless walker and explorer of rivers and mountains, Peacock was a conservationist almost two centuries ago and was in particular an *aficionado* of Welsh waterfalls. He arrived in North Wales in 1820, and his first stay was at Tremadoc, where William Maddocks was then undertaking his schemes to reclaim the estuary of the Glaslyn by building the giant sea-wall at Porthmadoc. Peacock then moved to the tiny village of Maentwrog which consisted of only seven houses, where Coleridge and a friend had lodged in 1794, to be totally captivated by the wild, unspoiled surroundings.

Peacock arrived in winter when the rivers are in zenith cry, charging off the mountains, falling into wild glens like torrents of spindrift snow or imprisoned in adamantine ice, when the sphagnum moss of the hillsides crackles underfoot like a gorseland fire. Like Coleridge before him, he intended to stay a few days only, but whereas the poet of 'Christabel' had managed to escape from the magic spell of the Welsh countryside after only a few days, Peacock remained in Maentwrog for many months (though no doubt the charms of Jane Gryffydh, daughter of the Ffestiniog rector, whom he was to marry eight years later, may have been a contributing factor).

His delight in the waterfalls and woodland of Merionethshire found first poetic expression in his 'Philosophy of Melancholy' which was published in 1812. Peacock celebrated the Merionethshire rivers and waterfalls round Maentwrog in dated heroic couplets but some of his period images still strike a ringing note.

In Part I of the poem, having described how 'The mighty cataracts burst and thunder down', the poem moves into what is unmistakably the wild Ganllwyd glen of Rhaeadr Ddu (The Black Waterfall, page 137) where

> The rock-set ash with tortuous branches grey
> Veils the deep glen and drinks the flying spray

and how Rhaeadr Ddu was struck dumb in full cry 'When winds were still and ice enchained the soil' and the arrested water had made 'A vast, fantastic crystal colonnade' where

> The scattering vapour frozen ere it fell
> With mimic diamonds spangled all the dell.

Rhaeadr Ddu exercised an irresistible lure for Peacock. He describes one visit to the waterfall in March 1820 to see the falls by moonlight when he was accompanied by his future father-in-law, Dr Gryffydh: 'The other day I prevailed on my new acquaintance Dr Griffith [*sic*] to accompany me to the *black cataract* a favourite haunt of mine about two and a half miles from here, at twenty minutes past eleven lighted by a full orbed moon. The effect was truly magnificent. The water descends from a mountain glen and precipitates itself in one sheet to foam over the black face into the capacious bar, the sides of which are all but perpendicular and covered with oak and hazel.' (The magic of the visit was somewhat marred by a near-fatal accident when Dr Gryffydh almost fell into the waterfall 'with a fall of fifteen feet perpendicular and but for an intervening hazel would have been infallibly hurled to the bottom.')

Peacock's novels, for which he is most remembered today, were filled with comedy and some biting satire. But always there shines his love of the Merionethshire scene, especially the waterfalls. As well as his description of Rhaeadr Ddu, Peacock has left a description of another Vale of Ffestiniog falls in his novel *Crotchet Castle* which is closely modelled on the Cynfal Waterfall (page 149). His father-in-law lived for some time at the house called Cynfal Fawr which was previously occupied by Huw Llwyd the 'wizard', who invoked the Devil from his midstream 'pulpit' near the Cynfal Waterfall.

'A cataract fell in a single sheet into the pool; the pool boiled and bubbled at the base of the fall, but through the greater part of its extent lay calm, deep, and black, as if the cataract had plunged through it to an unimaginable depth without disturbing its eternal repose. At the opposite extremity of the pool, the rocks almost met at their summits, the trees of the opposite banks almost intermingled with leaves, and another cataract plunged from the pool into a chasm on which the sunbeams never gleamed.'

Among more modern Welsh poets who have been captivated by the unique appeal of the waterfall, one who left a memorable poem on the subject was Gwent-born W. H. Davies, who passed his childhood in Newport, Monmouthshire, and is, in the opinion of many, the most under-estimated countryside voice of the twentieth century. Much of the nature poetry which Davies wrote is concerned with the closely observed wonder of small things, flower and leaf, the kingfisher and the adder, cowslips and primroses, glow-worms and sparrows, the lark on the wing. But in his poem 'The White Cascade' Davies forsakes the marvels of the miniscule and produces one of the most original waterfall images in the language. As in the case of Vaughan's waterfall, the exact provenance of the White Cascade is not known, though it fits with magic felicity the unnamed Snowdonia cataract falling down the mountainside of Cwm Merch (page 177). Here the white image, motionless because of distance, looks like a fall of snow on the mountain, though there is no direct evidence that the one-legged lyricist ever travelled in Snowdonia. The poem's master image of the waterfall as both bird and star enshrines the apotheosis of waterfall enchantment:

What happy mortal sees that mountain now,
The white cascade that's shining on its brow

The white cascade that's both a bird and star,
That has a ten-mile voice and shines as far?

Though I may never leave this land again,
Yet every spring my mind must cross the main

To hear and see that water-bird and star
That on the mountain sings, and shines so far.

For the poet Vernon Watkins, the waterfall is evocative of boyhood adventures. In his nostalgic poem 'Waterfalls' he writes how 'Always in that valley in Wales I hear the noise of waters falling' and how this brings back the memory of '. . . boys lost in the rookery's cries' as they search for nuts, '. . . branches cracking under their knees'.

The scenic splendours of Welsh waterfalls both north and south were also the cynosure of visiting artists, more especially during the closing phases of the eighteenth and the beginning of the nineteenth century, when the Continental 'Grand Tour' had been axed by the Napoleonic Wars. The waterfalls of Wales, its mountain summits and passes, woodlands, churches, ruined castles and mansions were the subjects of thousands of paintings, drawings and etchings by notable names. Some of the artists were hired by traveloguers, as for example in 1760 when the most famous travel-writer of the century, Thomas Pennant (1726-98) was accompanied on his expedition by his own watercolour artist, Moses Griffith, from the Lleyn Peninsular, just as today the journalist might be accompanied by a photographer. (Dr Johnson was loud in his praises of Pennant as a travel-writer).

Among the artists lured to Wild Wales from 1800 onwards were Richard Wilson, Inigo Richards, David Cox, Samuel Hieronymous Grimm, John 'Warwick' Smith,

Julius Caesar Ibbetson, Thomas Rowlandson, Henry Gastineau, Sir George Beaumont, John Ruskin and the young Turner. The latter was only twenty years of age when he made his first visit to South Wales, where he made many remarkable drawings, which included the Melincourt Falls (page 47) and the historic falls of Aberdulais (page 45). These drawings, incredibly accomplished for a youth of twenty, are in his South Wales sketchbook, in the British Museum. Among the artists mentioned above, John 'Warwick' Smith, so called because of the generous patronage of this artist by Lord Warwick, made a number of drawings of Hafod (page 113) and its waterfalls, near Devil's Bridge, which were subsequently produced in book form by a London publisher.

Turner was singled out by John Ruskin as the greatest ever painter of the *truth* of falling water and foaming torrents. Ruskin had an almost mystical concept of the primary beauty of water, comparable to the veneration of the Greeks, for whom water was one of the primary elements of creation. For Ruskin, water was the most wonderful of all 'inorganic substances', and the genius to capture the 'truth' of the waterfall was given to very few artists. To exemplify the difficulty of the challenge, he 'paints' a memorable if somewhat lavish word picture of a great waterfall, describing how.

> *The vault of water first bends, unbroken, in pure, polished velocity, over the arching rocks at the brow of the cataract, covering them with a dome of crystal twenty feet thick—so swift that its motion is unseen except when a foam globe from above darts over it like a falling star and how the trees are light, above it, under all their leaves at the instant that it breaks into foam, and how a jet of spray, leaps hissing out of the fall like a rocket, bursting in the wind and driven away in dust, filling the air with light: and how through the curdling wreaths of the restless crashing abyss below, the blue of the water paled by the foam in its body, shows purer than the sky through white rain-cloud . . .*

Apart from his praise of Turner as a waterfall artist, Ruskin singles out a painter named William Andrew Nesfield who painted many Welsh waterfalls and to whom he refers as 'Nesfield of the radiant cataract'. He describes him as 'a man of extraordinary feeling, both for the colour and the spirituality of a great waterfall, exquisitely delicate in his management of the changeful veil of spray and mist, just in his curves and contours . . . '.

In his discussion of waterfall painting, Ruskin surprisingly makes no mention of an artist named John Brandon Smith, one of the most successful painters of Welsh waterfalls whose principal period of exhibiting spanned the years 1848–84. John Brandon Smith became such a waterfall enthusiast that he was known among his contemporaries as 'Waterfall' Smith. In the past he has sometimes been confused with John Burrell Smith, who was also fond of painting streams and waterfalls. But Burrell Smith painted mostly in watercolours, 'Waterfall' Smith in oils, and connoisseurs of the genre judge him to be a consummate painter of Ruskin's waterfall 'truth'. Although he also painted falls in the Lake District and Scotland, his passion was for those of Wales, and during 1860–74 he exhibited paintings of Welsh waterfalls twelve times at the Royal Academy. Among his favourite rivers in North Wales were the Lledr and the Cynfal, but it was in the 'waterfall country' of the Vale of Neath that he found his richest source of subject. In particular he painted the falls of the Mellte (page 63), and like Turner he was also especially attracted by the historic falls on the River Dulais (page 45). Also among other paintings of the Neath Vale falls, there is one of Scŵd Gwladys (page 49) which is done in the style of the eighteenth-century English school and—somewhat optimistically perhaps—has been attributed to Gainsborough himself.

Among some extremely rare 'pieces' which feature the waterfalls of the Vale of Neath are a number of porcelain plates decorated with waterfall paintings executed by among others, Thomas Pardoe, the principal artist at the famous, if short-lived, 'Swansea Pottery' of the nineteenth century. They are collectors' pieces of rare beauty.

Among modern artists who have produced Welsh waterfall paintings in the 'modern vein', one can single out the Welsh artist Ceri Richards and in particular his memorable study of a 'Waterfall in Cardiganshire' now in the National Museum of Wales.

Waterfall Conquerors

It is a far cry from the lyrical appreciation of waterfalls by poets and painters to the waterfall world of the king of fish. If the migrating salmon fighting its way upstream to spawn could articulate, no doubt its judgement would savour little of the poet's and artist's pleasure but concentrate on the frustration offered by impassable falls where no salmon ladders have been installed to help its passage up its river of birth.

This immemorial contest of waterfall and salmon (and salmon-trout) is one of the great river dramas, which no poet has more graphically described than Andrew Young in one of the short, crystalline lyrics of which he was such a master. He paints a typical scene:

From rock-lipt lynn to lynn
Shaking the ferns and grasses with their din
The cascades overflow
And pour in pools to rise as boiling snow

Tossing their bodies bare
The salmon-trout are seen tasting our air
Far stronger is the flood
That rages in their few small drops of blood.

But how high can a fit salmon 'tasting the air', powered by the urge to procreate, leap in its attempt at water-conquest? It is a subject ripe for apochrypha, but the authenticated truth about these river athletes is startling enough. Salmon-watchers have documented a perpendicular leap of over eleven feet, the height being measured from the surface of the plunge pool to the pool above the falls. The leaping-power of a fish is affected by a number of factors. Just as the human high-jump specialist must have a good run-up before committing himself to the bar, so the salmon must have ample depth of water to achieve the necessary momentum before taking to the air. The optimum ratio of water depth to height of jump has been quantified as three to one, and to achieve the leap of over eleven feet mentioned above it is calculated that the salmon left the water at a vertical speed of twenty miles per hour from a pool thirty feet deep. Fortunately for the salmon, the need for a good depth of water to assist take-off is not often a limiting factor because the erosive power of the waterfall invariably 'excavates' the 'plunge pool' at the foot of the falls to a considerable depth.

Just as the salmon's leap demands a certain depth for take-off, so the maximum

The waterfall conqueror. The salmon migrating upstream to spawn in freshwater shallows has been known to make a jump of eleven feet over a waterfall.

attainable swimming speed depends on two principal factors: the body length of the individual fish and the temperature of the water. The fastest swimming speed of a big salmon is attained in water of higher temperatures. In his classic monograph on the *Design of Fish Passes,* Mr M. H. Beach of the MAFF Directorate of Fisheries Research writes, 'River temperatures can range from 0°C to about 25°C . . . Fish returning to their home river in June/July will encounter the highest temperature and will thus be capable of achieving the high swimming speeds necessary to surmount many of the more difficult obstructions. Later migrants, returning in October, will be facedwith lower temperatures and thus have a much reduced maximum speed.' The research also shows not merely that given the optimum temperature, the migratory fish is capable of achieving a surprisingly high swimming speed but also that its success in swimming up or leaping difficult waterfalls is associated with remarkable bursts of acceleration before take-off.

The salmon is the most spectacular conqueror of waterfall obstacles but there are other, comparable examples. The elvers, the tiny baby eels, on their way up river from the sea to populate the lakes and freshwater courses, ponds and ditches, provide an even greater *tour de force* than the salmon's leap. Salmon and eel spawning is in direct antithesis, for while the spawning salmon returns from the ocean to the river, the eels migrate from the river to the ocean to lay and fertilize their eggs. Eels living in freshwater may be seven years or over before they attain the sexual maturity indicated by their assumption of 'nuptial livery' which coats them with a silvery sheen. At maturity, they begin the astonishing saga of their journey to the sea, driven by an invincible urge to overcome all obstacles, even to the extent of bypassing the impassables by making detours through wet grass at night. Then, having reached the ocean, all the eels of the world head for the Sargasso Sea, the weird kingdom of weed floating off the continental shelf of Central America. There, in the darkness of the brown sargassum algae brought by storm winds from the West Indies and from Florida, which is massed in millions of tons on thousands of square miles of the warm, deeply saline ocean, the eels spawn and die. Immediately after hatching, the billions of tiny eel larvae rise from 500 to 300 fathoms, to begin their perilous current-borne journey eastwards, until, by their third year after hatching, they are approaching the coasts of Europe (others go to America). There the change from larvae to elvers is begun, until, as tiny, white baby eels encouraged by the decreasing salinity of the estuaries, they begin their long journeys up the tidal reaches of the river, carried forward with each successive tide, aided by their own corkscrew locomotion.

The ability of elvers to overcome waterfalls and obstacles in their journey to freshwater is legendary. To scale the waterfall they form a sort of living ladder on the rocks, moving upwards in an intertwining mass so that if the head of the ladder is broken by the water, part of the corporate strength of the mutually supporting line of elvers still remains. When the ascent proves impossible at a certain point, the elvers will continue their attempt to climb the falls elsewhere, seeking and finding other rocks to which they can cling and climb either in numbers or as individuals. It is an astonishing thought that all the eels found in the corrie lakes of Wales and elsewhere at an altitude perhaps of 2,000 feet have made the journey from the Sargasso Sea and may have overcome waterfalls that have defeated a fighting-fit forty-pound leaping salmon.

Apart from salmon and elvers, there is one other migrant, the weirdest creature that ever enters our rivers from the sea, for which the conquest of waterfalls is also a matter of life or death as a species. Salmon-watchers sometimes notice big adult salmon entering our Welsh rivers carrying deep scars on their flanks, obviously the sites of old wounds. The agents of these scars are sea-lampreys, powerful, sinuous eel-like creatures about three feet long. The sea-lamprey is an astonishing survivor of a remote stage in the evolution of vertebrates, with a single nostril on top of its head, a third or pineal eye which has no lens but is sensitive, like its tail, to light, and instead of jaws a round sucker which enables it to live a parasitic existence during its oceanic life. The sea-lamprey, which, like the salmon, has to spawn in freshwater, has a unique way of dealing with waterfall obstacles. The salmon leaps, and the elvers climb co-operatively but the sea-lamprey literally conquers the waterfall by suction, a technique which recalls the appropriateness of its Latin name-derivation of 'stone-sucker'. The strength of its sucker is such that it is literally impossible to separate it from its hold without breaking its body. With its hold maintained on the rock of the waterfall, the lamprey whips its body upwards and forward, at the same time releasing its suction to attach itself to another hold. Like the salmon, it is strong and powerful after its oceanic life of plentiful feeding.

In the negotiation of waterfalls the elvers and lampreys have to fend for themselves. It is only the salmon that demands and is offered help on its journey upstream. The design of the fish 'pass', the salmon 'ladder', is now a highly ingenious affair which takes account of all the complex factors involved, particularly the need to control the velocity of flow of the water in the fish 'pass'.

Finding the Waterfalls

The list of waterfalls given in the appendix on pages 229-32 includes all the waterfalls featured on the 1:50,000 Ordnance Survey maps of Wales and also contains a number of others not marked on these maps but judged worthy of inclusion.

The waterfalls are arranged in the book in two sections. Part I is an anthology of the finest and most interesting of the Welsh falls; those in Part II are in general not as dramatic but well worth a visit, especially after heavy rain.

Some waterfalls are quite easy to find, but others, especially the lesser-known ones, can be elusive and difficult. To facilitate the discovery of the chosen waterfall, the reader will find at the head of each chapter a number which corresponds to a number in the Appendix Reference List, from which the relevant Ordnance Survey map reference numbers can be obtained. (For most waterfall expeditions, especially to the more remote falls, strong boots and waterproofs are essential, also the relevant Ordnance Survey map and a compass.)

Having found the position on the map and arrived in the vicinity—often after nerve-testing progressions along steep, narrow lanes, it is always advisable, if possible, to make a local enquiry. (The public bar of a village pub can be a useful place to enquire.) You will often need all the help and information you can muster about the river concerned, the possible difficulties of access and the precise position of the falls. It is also vital to establish whether there is an approach along a public right of way. (Public rights of way are indicated on the Ordnance Maps by pink dots or dashes.) Where no such right of way is indicated, you should obviously, wherever possible, attempt to obtain permission. (Incidentally, you are not allowed to take cars on Forestry Commission roads, other than where authorized access is indicated.) The search for the waterfall can be hard and demanding, but success is infinitely rewarding. Determination is the name of the game.

Readers will note that three different Welsh generic terms for the waterfall have been used in the text. On the Ordnance Maps covering the Vale of Neath and its hinterland 'Scŵd', e.g. Scŵd Gwladys (the Gladys Waterfall), is used. The word is a variant form of 'Ysgŵd', which signifies 'fall', 'flow' or, possibly (again locally), 'fling'. This Welsh term may share a common Low German derivation with the English word 'scud'.

As one moves from the south, two other terms are found on the Ordnance Maps, prefacing the name of the waterfall: 'Rhaeadr', e.g. Rhaeadr Ddu (the Black Waterfall), which is sometimes misspelt 'Rhaiadr', the 'Pistyll', e.g. 'Pistyll y Llyn (the Waterfall of the Lake).

Those waterfalls without names appear as either a singular or plural use of the word. The term 'waterfall' indicates a single fall, usually some distance from its nearest neighbour. The plural 'waterfalls' signifies either a series of closely adjacent waterfalls or a series of cascades, i.e. very small falls.

The term 'waterfall(s)' is used by the Ordnance to embrace all unnamed falling-water phenomena, whether falling more or less perpendicularly off a cliff or crag, down a hillside or mountain or along a rocky river bed. (In descriptive writing—though never on maps—the word 'cataract' is sometimes used for a big descent of water down a mountainside.) But there is no quantitative definition. Whether a particular example of falling water qualifies for map inclusion as 'waterfall(s)' or not is decided by the Ordnance Survey cartographer on the spot.

In examining the Ordnance maps of Wales to pinpoint the position of waterfalls, particularly in the hill and mountain areas, the reader will frequently encounter the word 'hafod' or, more rarely, 'hafodty' or 'meifod'. The word epitomizes a one-time Welsh pastoral way of life based on the seasonal migration of stock from the lowlands to the hills during the summer season. The permanent lowland homestead was known in Wales as the 'hendre', and each spring, when the cultivation in the lowlands was completed, the lowland homestead, humans and livestock alike, moved to the temporary upland 'hafod' where the livestock could graze to the top of the unenclosed mountain, turning the grass into salted butter, cheese and livestock increase. In the autumn, the farming unit returned to the lowland 'hendre'. This system of seasonal livestock and human migration, known as 'transhumance', is still practised in Switzerland and parts of Scandinavia and continued in some Welsh mountainous areas into the nineteenth century. Then came the Enclosures, and the statutory fencing of common land transformed the remote 'hafod' in the hills of Wales into a self-contained high-altitude farm.

These historical factors coupled with the curious absence of primogeniture in the Welsh property-inheritance laws resulted in the establishment of hundreds of Welsh hill farmsteads, 'hafodau', most of them now abandoned and many hardly more than heaps of stones. But as one searches the maps for the waterfalls one finds a moving cartographical testimony of how the hard, 'hafod' way of life, the subsistence vicissitudes and the lonely distances which separated remote mountain neighbours and eventually destroyed it, failed to dim or extinguish the Welsh love of the poetic image in verse and song which has remained such a cardinal feature of Welsh rural life. The environs of Welsh waterfalls can provide a rich harvest of evidence of these colourful names. The hinterland of the Hengwm Waterfall on the edge of Plynlimon is a typical example, rich with evocative titles: Esgair y Gog (Crag of the Cuckoo), Llyn-y-Delyn (Lake of the Harp), Coed Cerrig Brithion (Wood of the Speckled Stones),

Banc-yr-Wyn (The Lamb's Hillside), Nant Rhyd Wen (Brook of the White Ford). There are hundreds of other examples over the hills and mountains of Wales.

The Hengwm, surrounded by these typically graphic descriptions, is one of the Welsh waterfalls that freezes in hard winters. More than any other factor, freezing accentuates the picturesque individuality which is one of the great appeals of waterfalls. For example, when an iron frost removes all remaining foliage from the dell, Pistyll Cain is transformed into a sculpted succession of ice terraces which have long presented a formidable challenge to technical climbers. The quartzite cornice of the frozen Scŵd Gwladys is charmingly decorated with hanging flounces of ice, which seem entirely appropriate to its feminine name. Waterfalls in winter are most likely to be struck dumb in mid-air when they face due north or are sited in frost pockets, into which the frosty air flows down like the water (the so-called 'katabatic factor'). Finding the remote frozen waterfall can present a stiffer challenge (for the hardy well-equipped searcher) because there is no vocal announcement from the frozen falls to indicate its presence.

(For those unaccustomed to using Ordnance Survey maps the following example of how to find the route to the waterfall entered on the Distribution of Waterfalls Map may be helpful. Having selected, say, waterfall number 57, turn to the Appendix List and read off the information given opposite that number. You will find this waterfall is on Ordnance Survey map number 125 in the SJ area of that map and that the 'easting' number is 073 and the 'northing' number is 296. A clear exposition of these two terms is given in the margin of every Ordnance map. The waterfall—which in this instance is named Pistyll Rhaeadr, the highest in Wales—will therefore be found on map 125 at the point where the two imaginary grid lines, drawn through the 'easting' and 'northing' points, intersect.)

The Farewell Falls

Over the past decades a number of fine Welsh waterfalls have been extinguished or debilitated by the demands of industry, electricity generation and the domestic needs of urban populations in England and Wales, though Welsh waterfalls have not been tampered with on a tithe of the scale of Welsh lakes. It is never other than a shock to reach a lonely and lovely lake in a remote Welsh cwm, probably after walking through an area of outstanding natural beauty, to encounter the tell-tale dams, leets and conduits which signify the tarnishing of yet another countryside gem. It is, I suppose, only too easy to become emotional about the fate of so many Welsh lakes, hard even not to see it as the vandalizing of irreplaceable masterpieces. The truth is , of course, that in an age of increasing population and living-standard expectations, the most we can realistically fight for is to ensure that the needs and provision of water and power now and for the future are satisfied with minimum damage to our irreplaceable environment.

But, like the lakes, waterfalls can pay the price of 'progress', and some notable examples leap to mind. The A543 road near Pentrefoelas on the A5 runs across the pectoral sweeps of remote Denbighshire moorlands, where the contours of Mynydd Hiraethog are bright with mile upon mile of flowering heather, with the River Aled running between. The Aled is a tributary of the Elwy, about which Gerald Manley Hopkins wrote the famous poem which begins

> Lovely the woods, waters, meadows, combes, vales,
> All the air things wear that build this world of Wales

and then goes on to castigate the human element as the blot on the beautiful Welsh landscape!

The Aled has its source in Llyn Aled and after half a mile enters Llyn Aled Isaf. These two lakes are now both reservoirs, while to the south there is another large man-made lake, the conifer-fringed Alwen reservoir, three miles long and half a mile wide. Until the impounding of the Llyn Aled and Aled Isaf lakes, the Aled river issuing from the latter produced one of the most dramatic waterfalls in Wales, its white skeins of water lighting up hundreds of feet of rock as it fell into a deep, dark ravine. It is an especially sombre, even menacing gorge, a fact reflected in the grim nomenclature of the waterfall which was named Rhaeadr y Bedd (Waterfall of the Grave). The magnificent falls have now totally disappeared, replaced by a valve-controlled release of water when required, from the side of the reservoir, with the inevitable accompanying ugliness of dam walls and aprons of concrete. Without the waterfall the gorge is depleted, denuded, almost dead, for white water is the most dramatic sign of Nature moving about her business of change.

Other Welsh waterfalls have disappeared not because of reservoir needs but because the rivers have been subjugated for power, especially when they were associated with the power-gradients of hanging valleys. In the early days, the rivers and waterfalls of hanging valleys would be harnessed for driving waterwheels, with minimal or even no damage to the scene. But the power-demands of turbines are of a different order. Dolgarrog, a village some eight miles south of Conwy, is now the location of a huge aluminium works, sited at this point because of the water which could be harnessed from the corrie lakes of Llyn Eigiau and Llyn Cowlyd (the latter one of the deepest in Wales, with a maximum depth of 222 feet). Before the installation of the Dolgarrog hydro-electric water scheme, the rivers Porthllwyd and Ddu fell into Nant Conwy in magnificent waterfalls, famous throughout North Wales. The drama of the Porthllwyd cataract can be envisaged when one realizes that the river—thanks partly to a fault zone—falls over 700 feet in less than a quarter of a mile into the valley below. (There was a tragic loss of sixteen lives in 1925 when the dam on Llyn Eigiau was breached and its waters engulfed the village.)

The waterfalls have gone but there still remains one particular spot on the River Porthllwyd formerly associated with its waterfall which is still well worth a visit (apart from the lake). It occurs just before the river begins its descent into the present reservoir down the precipitous gorge. To reach it, turn left just before the bridge over the river at the village of Talybont (about a mile from Dolgarrog), to climb a drastically narrow, steep lane with few passing places until the road flattens out before arriving at a gateway marked 'No Parking', the entrance to an unoccupied sheep farmstead, still in frequent use for sheep gathering and handling. Park by the little bridge a hundred yards from the gate and, returning, cross over a stile almost hidden in the hedge, which takes you across sidelands covered with bracken high above the noisy river. (If you make the visit in late autumn, there is the extra dividend of a feast of purpling wild plums from nearby trees.) After four more stiles, you arrive within a few yards of the river. This is the point where the Porthllwyd begins its precipitous drop.

It is a place to stand and stare, or sit and contemplate, a miniature grotto, a tiny gem where the water enters through 'Porthllwyd', the 'Grey Portal' of rock which gives the river its name, into a tiny palace of polished stone, overshadowed by silver birch trees which in the late autumn shower the rocks with gold sovereigns among a wealth of ferns and bryophytes. As often happens with Welsh cataracts, the river seems to be enjoying a last moment of pause and peace before committing itself irretrievably to the drama of descent where the once tumultuous waterfall is now a fading memory.

Geologists speak of the waterfall as a 'temporary phenomenon' in our landscapes.

But the phrase has no relevance to the time-span of human mortality. The concept of a lack of permanence is strictly in a geological context, and in the world of waterfalls 'temporary' may have a connotation of thousands or even millions of years.

Waterfalls are so described because it is the *modus operandi* of rivers to seek the elimination of all gross geological discordinances, the removal of all obstacles such as waterfalls which stand in the way of the ultimate achievement of its equilibrium, the production of a relatively smooth, upward-concave profile.

Paradoxically the river's principal agent for the removal of the waterfall is the waterfall itself. The logic is simple. Waterfalls are the river's most powerful erosion agents, though of course their power will vary, depending especially on the height and water volume of the falls, the particular rock formation, and the degree of perpendicularity of the falling water. The erosive power can be realized if one thinks that a river falling more or less freely over a cliff of, say, 250 feet will have attained a theoretical velocity of ninety miles an hour when it hits the plunge pool at the foot of the falls, though in practice the waterfall, whatever its height, can seldom be treated as a freely falling body, for there are factors of internal friction, the effect of wind and others. But the erosive power is still very great even in the case of a relatively low fall.

This erosive power of the waterfall can lead to its own eventual elimination in one of two ways. Firstly, this can be achieved by the 'migration' of the waterfall upstream through the headward erosion of the cliff or scarp, the process exemplified by Scŵd yr Eira. In the fullness of time, as this waterfall moves progressively further and further upstream towards the mountain source of the Hepste, the falls will slowly but surely assume a lower profile and eventually be reduced to the form of rapids which in turn will be graded out by the erosive power of the tumbling water itself. Or secondly, the erosion may act in a downstream direction to bevel the entire section of river which contains the falls.

But the time-scale of this death through its own power, this suicide by majesty, which is the eventual fate of all waterfalls, is impossible for mere mortals to conceive and appreciate. As far as we are concerned—assuming we do not plunder them for power or otherwise destroy them, the splendour of Welsh waterfalls is forever.

Part I

The Aberdulais Falls (1)

A historian of the town of Neath and its environs once wrote that during the late eighteenth century there were only two subjects which commanded the attention of more artists than the Aberdulais Falls. The first was Windsor Castle, part of which dated back to William the Conqueror, the second was Emma, Lady Hamilton, the beautiful mistress of Lord Nelson.

The much-painted and lauded falls of Aberdulais, now owned by the National Trust, are formed by the River Dulais which rises near Onllwyn, not far from the source of the River Pyrddin. For much of its course the Dulais flows through a surprisingly wide U-shaped valley floor, mostly marginal farming land, between the 800- and 900-foot contours. The position of the falls is about half a mile before the Dulais meets the Neath, about three miles north-west of the town of that name in West Glamorgan.

The Aberdulais Waterfall is associated with one of the many faults and fractures in this part of South Wales which have given the rivers access to the softer shales. At the same time the faulting near Aberdulais has thrown up massive arch-like (anticlinal) folds which, though smaller, bear a striking resemblance to the classic anticline called Bwa Maen by the entrance to the River Sychryd gorge near the village of Pont Nedd Fechan. The waterfalls begin when the broad-flowing Dulais, with a precision as though it were falling over a man-made weir, charges over a bar of rock across the river bed. The falling water searches out a big recess to the left which it fills with foam before making its huge tumble into the plunge pool below, thundering down in a mountain of foam over the massive rocky outcrops.

Of all the works of art painted at the Aberdulais falls in the nineteenth century, many were elaborately executed in oils but it is the pencil drawings of Turner, then only twenty years old, which most graphically and faithfully capture the distinctive curling roll of the descending flood. (A famous painting purporting to be of Aberdulais, by the artist John Brandon Smith, who was one of its most prolific painters, is almost certainly the Scŵd yr Eira Waterfall in the Vale of Neath). There is an annexe near the falls where the National Trust has collected some of the work of earlier visiting artists.

To see the Aberdulais Falls in full flow is to appreciate the enormous power which once made the environs of this particular waterfall a major centre of metal-processing in Wales. Although there were rudimentary coal-mines and ironworks in the Neath hinterland earlier, one of the first major copper-processing operations followed the establishment of a smelting and refinery works in the proximity of the Aberdulais falls. The ores for Aberdulais were brought from Cornwall in small ships up the Bristol Channel. The Aberdulais falls remained a giant workhorse for various metal production processes in this part of Wales well into the nineteenth century.

The Aberdulais Waterfall, a favourite scene for visiting artists for over two centuries.

The Melincourt Waterfall (3)

The Melincourt Waterfall (the name is the anglicized form of Melin-y-Cwrt, the Mill of the Court) is most conveniently approached through the small town of Resolven, along the road from Glyn Neath to Neath.

Pass through the town until a marked public footpath to the waterfall leaves the main road a few hundred yards south-west of the Resolven pensioners' hall. The transition of scene is immediate and astonishing. From a landscape pocked and heaped with the scars and detritus of two centuries of industry and mining, you move into the lush green gloaming of the unspoiled Melincourt combe. The early path to the falls leads along the side of the stream, through a narrow gorge, until the ravine begins to broaden out as you near the falls.

Advertising its roar, the waterfall suddenly appears when the Melincourt brook cascades from a height of eighty feet down its dark wall of rock. Round the base of the falls today are strewn huge piles of rock-fall boulders with the astonishing symmetrical rectangular shape of 'jointed' rocks which have broken off and which tell the story of a waterfall in a state of recession. These rockfalls were once part of the overhanging conglomerate of rock, at a time when one could walk behind the waterfall, as one can with Scŵd yr Eira and Scŵd Gwladys today.

The Melincourt Falls were harnessed through a huge 'overshot' waterwheel which powered the tilt-hammer used in the iron furnaces to produce pig iron for the nearby tinplate industry. The furnaces were fed by charcoal, manufactured from native oak nearby, and the demand of industry was mainly responsible for decimating the woodlands of the immediate environment and over a wide area of native woodlands. It took the timber from three acres of woodland—mostly hardwoods—to produce enough charcoal to make just one ton of iron in those days. 'Charcoal iron', like the produce from the furnaces of the Melincourt, was the basis of the South Wales tin industry.

Despite their industrial history, the Melincourt Falls and their woodlands environs were, and still are today, a happy hunting ground for botanists. In the elm and lime woodlands, despite the increasing pollution of industry, many relatively rare plants still flourish, St John's wort, royal fern,, the butterworts and beech polypoidy, as well as numerous liverworts and mosses. The richest habitat is near the waterfall itself, where the water draining from the limestone provides a source of mineral nutrients in conditions of high, constant humidity. But one would be hard put to find today the wild strawberries which were once a delicious dividend of a walk up the Melincourt waterfall combe.

The Melincourt Waterfall, set in the green gloaming of an unspoiled coombe, in the heart of industrial South Wales.

Scŵd Gwladys (9)

(The Gladys Falls)

The village of Pont Nedd Fechan (linguistically vandalized to Pontneathvaughan) is sited just over a mile from the small town of Glyn Neath in West Glamorgan. It lies in the confluence area of a number of Vale of Neath rivers and is the best departure point for a visit to Scŵd Gwladys, one of the Vale's popular waterfalls, which occurs on the River Pyrddin.

The route to the waterfall begins behind the Angel Inn in Pont Nedd Fechan, where you turn left onto the west bank of the Nedd Fechan. For much of the walk the river roars along its water-sculpted passage of rock folds and anticlines thirty feet below with massive curtains of ivy falling in lianoid chaos down to the white water. About a mile from the inn you reach an iron girder bridge at the confluence of the Pyrddin and Nedd Fechan. This is where the ascent proper of the Pyrddin begins, to take us to a frontal encounter with Scŵd Gwladys. Leaving the girder bridge on the right, continue upstream following a marked path to a recently constructed viewing-point where Scŵd Gwladys can be seen in all its grace and beauty. This is the end of the path, and to get nearer you have to do a certain amount of scrambling and walking. For some, Scŵd Gwladys is one of the most beautiful falls in the Vale.

Gwladys is approximately forty feet high, falling over a cornice of hard, erosion-resistant quartzite which spans over half the width of the ravine. Except in times of exceptional flood, the Pyrddin falls mainly over the left-hand section of the ledge for, due to a fault, the rock strata have a slight tilt to the south-west. As a consequence of this inclination the river has cut more deeply into the south-west bank of the ravine, and the north-east pavement of rock over which the Pyrddin formerly flowed is bare except for the grasses—and in places small bushes—which have colonized the soil, and debris carried down the slopes by the river in times of flood.

Like its sister, Scŵd yr Eira, Scŵd Gwladys is a waterfall in a state of recession. Here too, over the aeons, the black friable shale at the base of the falls has been washed away, and the progressive undermining of the erosion-resistant quartzite overhang causes it to break away at one of its 'joints' to leave a more or less vertical cliff face. It is also possible to walk behind the Gwladys falls. But the tilt of the strata means that Scŵd Gwladys is also moving laterally as well as upstream.

During the nineteenth century Scŵd Gwladys was anglicized into 'the Lady's Falls' and may be still so described. To change Gwladys into 'Lady's' is an understandable English adaptation, but it has been suggested also that the grace of the falls, with the water falling like a billowing skirt, may well have helped the semantic distortion to gain currency.

Scŵd Gwladys where the River Pyrddin falls over a hard cornice of sandstone which has a tilt to the south-west so that the river flows over a section of the cornice.

Scŵd Einion Gam (8)

(Waterfall of the Crooked Anvil)

Scŵd Einion Gam is the second principal waterfall on the River Pyrddin and occurs about a mile up river from its point of girder-bridge confluence with the River Nedd Fechan. So the initial approach to Einion Gam is as for Scŵd Gwladys, with the journey beginning behind the Angel Inn at Pont Nedd Fechan.

At the iron bridge, instead of continuing straight on as for the Gwladys falls, cross the bridge to the other side and follow the path to the left along the base of the steep, tree-clad slope. In a straight line Scŵd Einion Gam is about half a mile up river from the bridge, but almost twice that distance has to be covered because of the intermittent difficulties of access. After a few hundred yards of initial walk and scramble, you arrive on the tilted glaciated pavement above the Gwladys Waterfall where there is a large landmark stone sometimes called 'the Logan' and a superb view downstream over the cornice of the waterfall.

For a short distance from this point the route is relatively easy, sometimes taking in strips of meadow and easily negotiated ledges of rock. Then progress becomes painfully slow, for in places the bank disappears and the towering cliffs fall perpendicularly into the river, necessitating a crossing and recrossing of the river to the opposite bank. This demands great care when the river is high, and it is dangerous when the river is in flood.

Rounding the last bend in the bed of the white-flecked water brings one face to face with Scŵd Einion Gam falls where they drop down eighty feet of tree-shrouded black rock into the plunge pool below. The river falls over another ledge of rock about fifteen feet from the foot of the main falls.

Technically, like so many waterfalls in the Vale of Neath, Scŵd Einion Gam is associated with a fault—a crack in the crustal rocks—which has exposed the middle band of soft shale and brought it into contact with the river so that the Pyrddin has eaten away the soft deposits, with the increasing overhang of hard rock breaking off where joints occur, leaving a more or less sheer drop into the deep ravine. Just over half-way down its cliff the river is deflected by a protuberance of hard rock which has probably given the waterfall its name. 'Gam' is a mutated form of the Welsh word 'cam', signifying crooked.

Scŵd Einion Gam (difficult to approach because the river has to be forded several times) falls obliquely down an eighty-foot cliff and is related to a geological fault.

Scŵd yr Eira (13)

(The Waterfall of Snow)

Scŵd yr Eira is the widely acclaimed waterfall superstar of the Vale of Neath. It occurs on the River Hepste, which has its origins in the Red Sandstone mass of Fforest Fawr (the Great Forest) where three small streams unite to form the river.

The waterfall has been a source of wonder and admiration for a long time. In 1823 a topographical survey of *England and Wales Illustrative of Natural and Local History* recorded that, 'The most remarkable natural object in Brecknockshire is the fall of the river Hepste in an extremely wild and romantic glen. The whole sheet of the river rushes so precipitously over a stupendous rock as to form a complete arch of water . . . [this] noble cascade dashing in furious foam on to its stoney bed, throwing up clouds of spray and deafening the ear with its complaints.'

When there is a lot of water, the River Hepste falls in 'furious foam' over the precipice as a monolithic curtain of white, falling well clear of the rocks below, and the plunge pool of Scŵd yr Eira has been deepened by the action of stones being whirled round and round by the weight of water into the deepest pool on the river. But in drought, the fifty-foot-high Scŵd yr Eira completely changes its nature. Then it distils a sound of gently falling water, separating as it falls into three distinct streams which shimmer over the cliff in a lacy triad of cascades. On a sunny day the streams are shot through with tinges of ochre and gold which mingle with the green of the giant stalactites of moss, the crystal liverworts and the other semi-squatic plants which hang on the cliff behind the falls. In sunlight, the sunbeams, which strike the light spray as the cascades hit the fronting steps of hard rock, fracture into rainbows and turn the scene into an artist's dream.

The recess formed behind the waterfall through the eating away of the soft shale at the base from the splash of falling water (page 16) has become Scŵd yr Eira's most famous distinguishing feature which continues to lure and delight adults and children alike. At the present time there is a recess about ten feet deep where one can walk behind the waterfall to the other bank of the river. If you walk behind the falls during low water, the trio of streams is metamorphosed into long chains of luminous waterdrops through which the grotto and the view downstream are seen through a gold and silver haze. Old prints show shepherds driving their flocks behind the Scŵd yr Eira falls to the other side of the valley, and indeed when the river is full, this is the only way to cross to the other bank without deep wading.

The setting of Scŵd yr Eira matches its grace and symmetry, for through cutting into the soft shale the sides of the ravine have been widened by the river into a grotto.

Like its other sister rivers of the Vale of Neath, Hepste in its southward journey when it reaches the Carboniferous limestone, disappears underground a number of

---

Scŵd yr Eira, one of the superstars of the Vale of Neath, falls in a graceful aqueous arch over the cliff, with a rocky walkway behind the falls.

times. The course of the Hepste for almost three miles is along the Carboniferous limestone belt and for part of its course is so continuously dry that weeds thrive amongst the stones of the river bed. About three-quarters of a mile above Scŵd yr Eira the Hepste produces a first small waterfall when the river falls over a bed of sandstone in the Millstone Grit and also makes its first disappearance into the fissured limestone. But after heavy rain, when the water comes sheeting into the upper gorge and the beds of Millstone Grit and Coal Measures afford no fissures or faults for it to escape, the underground limestone caverns are quickly filled and the river comes to life again and begins to flow on the surface.

The approach to Scŵd yr Eira has now been made much easier by the Neath authorities (as has the approach to the other waterfalls in the valley). The best approach is from the village of Penderyn, turning left after the Lamb Inn, following the old mineral railway line to a derelict quarry on the northern slopes of Foel Penderyn and then striking a little west of north over the moorland, following the fence until you reach the twin 'glacial erratics' near the head of the descent gully to the waterfall. Alternatively you can reach Scŵd yr Eira from the Forestry car-park by Porth yr Ogof Cave, by following the path along the bank of the Mellte.

Several times in this book, Scŵd yr Eira and the Niagara Falls have appeared side by side, which may seem an inappropriate juxtaposition, even though the actual comparison content is of course concerned with geomorphological processes. But Scŵd yr Eira can hold up its head as perfect of its kind, in striking harmony with its own landscape.

A close-up of the falls from the recess behind the waterfall.

The Lower Cilhepste Falls (12)

No river in the Vale of Neath celebrates its last few hundred yards of independent life in more defiantly boisterous style than the Hepste. For perhaps fifty yards after its performance at Scŵd yr Eira it flows along a relatively flat river bed. Then quite suddenly it begins the most dramatically sustained performance of its course.

At the end of the Scŵd yr Eira grotto the Hepste begins to fall down a gorge which rapidly becomes steeper and more precipitous so that the river gathers more and more momentum. The river drops over a hundred feet in the first furlong of fall, roaring between the sides of the ravine and over the massive outcrops along its bed. In the last few hundred yards it falls another 250 feet. The totality of these waterfalls and cascades produced in the Hepste's terminal plunge is known as the Lower Cilhepste Falls.

The distinctive step-like character of the river's approach to its confluence with the Mellte river is due partly to faulting in the strata and partly to the fact that Hepste forms a hanging valley relative to the Mellte. The fault is the same one which gives rise to the Scŵd Clungwyn Isaf fall on the Mellte, and affords both rivers access to the softer deposits, to sharpen their gradient of flow.

This final phase of the Hepste's career was probably given its name of Lower Cilhepste Falls to distinguish it from the Upper Cilhepste Falls, the name by which the waterfall Scŵd yr Eira was originally known. Both took their names from a group of farms in this part of the Vale of Neath, Cilhepste Coed (Cilhepste Wood), Cilhepste Cerrig (Cilhepste Stones) and Cilhepste Bach (Little Cilhepste), just as the various Clungwyn Falls on the Mellte also owe their names to a local farm.

There is a picturesque avenue of approach from which to view the Lower Cilhepste Falls. You can pass behind the Scŵd yr Eira waterfall and then walk a short way downstream on the northern bank until you encounter the steep path to the right which leads eventually to the Scŵd yr Pannwr. But instead of continuing to the forestry plantation fence as for Pannwr, you should take a steep path to the left which leads down to the Hepste below the final waterfall of the Lower Cilhepste complex. But the barrier of hard rock over which it makes its final plunge after the velocity-gathering descent through the ravine presents the walker with a virtually inaccessible barrier to making the return upstream along the river bank. So you have to climb the steep scree through a fine display of sessile oaks to the path above, from which you can again follow the thundering white course of the river through the trees and at a later stage descend again to the river. From its last waterfall the Hepste has but a short distance before its confluence with the Mellte.

A short distance below Scŵd yr Eira, the River Hepste begins its final (hanging valley) descent to the Mellte and forms a dramatic series of waterfalls.

The Waterfalls of the Nedd Fechan (10, 11, 14)

(Little Neath)

The River Nedd Fechan rises between Fan Nedd and Fan Gyhirych and, after flowing southwards to receive the River Pyrddin, flows on to its confluence with the Mellte below Pont Nedd Fechan. From this point it is known as the River Neath.

Like its sister rivers of the Vale which cross mixed geological strata, it too flows from hard rock, Millstone Grit, across a belt of Carboniferous limestone where it sinks underground, in this case at Pwll y Rhyd, where it has carved out an underground system of caves.

In any area other than the Vale of Neath, with its many great waterfalls, the Nedd Fechan would be famous, for along two miles of its course it produces numerous falls of diversity and charm, with distinctive features found nowhere else in the Vale. The principal waterfall section of the river lies between its point of confluence with the Pyrddin and the Forestry Commission car-park and picnic place at Pont Melin Fach. It is an exciting stretch of water with a series of rewards for the waterfall-hunter.

The best approach to this stretch of river is to proceed as for Scŵd Gwladys and Scŵd Einion Gam from behind the Angel Inn at Pont Nedd Fechan. Then cross the girder bridge at the confluence of Pyrddin and Nedd Fechan and keep to the right bank of the Nedd Fechan. It is an easy path, though much of it in the early stages runs high above the river, which is more or less inaccessible at the bottom of precipitous screes colonized by a wealth of trees, ash, birch, wych elm, oak, beech and some small lime trees which in places cling precariously to their footing, seeming to grow out of the rock itself at impossible angles. In summer the numerous trees mean that the river is almost obscured by foliage in places.

In its course from the girder bridge the river produces a number of cascades and rapids, before the occurrence of its first named display known as the Horseshoe Falls. Here the river, after a boisterous approach of about a hundred yards over a hard sandstone pavement, pours over a curving ledge of rock, then falls over a second ledge where it is channelled between two small, naturally occurring breakwaters of sandstone, protruding from each bank of the river, before continuing its course downstream. The effect is most attractive, a series of graceful curves as though the passage of the river had been landscaped over a planned semi-circular ledge.

The Horseshoe Falls are near a small footbridge which crosses a feeder tributary of Nedd Fechan. The little bridge carries a plaque which announces that this is Pont Nant Llechau. The materials for the bridge in a partly assembled form were lifted to the spot by helicopter from nearby Gwernblaedde Farm and dropped near the tributary gully. It is possible to scramble down to the river to the hard sandstone pavement fronting the Horseshoe Falls.

The Upper Ddwli waterfall falls almost parallel to the flow of the Nedd Fechan.

The Horseshoe Falls are as it were the *hors d'œuvre* of the feast impending up river. The two main Nedd Fechan falls occur where the river has cut ledges in the hard Millstone Grit deposits. By custom the two main waterfalls are known as the 'Upper Ddwli' and the 'Lower Ddwli', though the Ordnance map records only the 'Ddwli' waterfall, which is the upper of the two main falls. The Lower Ddwli is a two-stage waterfall. The main fall tumbles thirty feet down a sheer cliff cut in the Millstone Grit, falling onto a fronting pavement. The river then continues along one side of the sandstone pavement due to a slight tilt in the strata, before falling over another wide ledge. Only in flood does the Nedd Fechan occupy more than half the pavement, so that one can walk over almost the whole of it. On the left side which is not washed by the river, the leaf and soil debris falling down the slopes has built up, to be colonized by trees and shrubs. The whole area is, as it were, a wide proscenium of rock where the river is only a partial tenant. It is possible to scramble down to the pavement both above and below the falls, and the top vantage-point provides an impressive view downstream into the wooded ravine of the Nedd Fechan.

About a furlong further upstream, the next waterfall, the Upper Ddwli, can be seen through the trees, not far from the picnic place of Pont Melin Fach. Unlike its sister waterfall which pours over a ledge at almost right angles to the river, Upper Scwd Ddwli falls over a ledge almost parallel to the course of the river. In one respect the Upper Ddwli earns a top accolade in the vale. There is no waterfall setting in the whole of the Vale of Neath which wears the light of the setting autumn sun with more splendour than that of the Upper Ddwli. Perhaps it is the angle at which the lengthening sunbeams strike the curtain of water, set against the yellowing foliage of the surrounding trees. The birch leaves begin to fall early, and in autumn the glaciated pavement is starred with gold. It recalls the delightful stanza from Andrew Young's poem 'The Salmon Leap':

> Leaves, and not birds, now flit
> Brighter than yellow wagtail and cole-tit
> Or on the water lie
> Making a sunset of the fishes' sky.

In autumn the scene at the Lower Ddwli can resemble a Japanese painting.

Scŵd Clungwyn (17)

(Waterfall of the White Meadow)

Few rivers in Wales in the course of a comparably short life give rise to more dramatic waterfall variety than the River Mellte in the Vale of Neath. The name translates as 'the River of Lightning', and for much of its life it certainly lives up to the promise of thunder as it falls and foams through its succession of steep-sided glens. Yet like all its sister rivers of the Vale, Mellte vanishes from sight in places, falling through limestone fissures and roaring underground for hundreds of yards through the spectacular netherworld of the Porth yr Ogof (Gateway of the Cave) system of caves (page 67).

Porth yr Ogof is sited south of the little village of Ystradfellte and is a convenient spot from which to visit the main Mellte waterfalls. There is a Forestry Commission car-park near the cave; from here cross the road to follow the field track southwards on the eastern bank of the Mellte which leads to a footbridge. Then cross to the west bank where almost immediately the voice of the first waterfall announces its presence.

Scŵd Clungwyn, sometimes called 'the Upper Clungwyn Falls', is found here because a geological fault in the hard sandstone and Millstone Grit has given the river access to the soft, middle-band shales, and the particular section of fault with which the falls is associated is discernible from the western side just above the waterfall. The differential erosion ensuing has produced a two-step waterfall, falling initially onto a rocky ledge with a subsequent descent down a second vertical face, a leap of fifty feet. Above the falls the river flows over a wide sandstone 'pavement' on which one can walk to the head of the falls. The concentration of water to one side of the waterfall cliff, due to the tilt of the sandstone strata to the south-east, has resulted in deeper erosion on the steeper south-easterly cliffs of the gorge. In this respect Scŵd Clungwyn repeats the differential erosion pattern of Scŵd Gwladys where the south-westerly tilt of the strata has also produced deeper erosion and steeper cliffs on that side of the valley.

This Mellte waterfall is, of course, most impressive when the river is full. But it has a very distinctive charm at low water when the river falls like singing embroidery over the south-west ledge.

Scŵd Clungwyn, which is about a mile and three-quarters south of Ystradfellte, can also be approached by the road from the village of Pont Nedd Fechan towards Ystradfellte. Cars can be parked on the wide verges about two hundred yards south of Capel Hermon (there is also a shop and a petrol station). The path to the Mellte leads through a gate, over a stile and a shallow ford, past deserted farm buildings until the waterfalls are heard in the valley below.

Scŵd Clungwyn, in dry weather, showing how, because of the nature of the fault, the water gathers towards the south-east side of the ledges.

Scŵd Isaf Clungwyn (16)
(Lower White Meadow Waterfall)

Scŵd Isaf Clungwyn has been known and eulogized for centuries. A late eighteenth-century traveloguer, Richard Warner, typifies the lyrical awe with which early writers described the scene:

> *. . . a series of connected waterfalls forming one whole of inconceivable grandeur. The flood enlarged to an uncommon degree by the deluge of rain and pent up within a channel too narrow for its increased bulk tore over the rocks and rushed from ledge to ledge with a fury that produced a sensation . . . as if the whole atmosphere around were agitated and the solid foundation of the rock were shaken under one's feet. The rage of the torrent was such as to completely divest it during its descent of the appearance of water. All was vapour, foam and wild confusion.*

Warner was describing the spectacle from the west bank, and this is still the best viewing vantage-point at any time of year. I have visited the waterfall at all seasons, in winter when it was a roaring mountain of water cannonading into the gorge, in summer when it makes a shimmering tracery over the dark jagged rocks. It never gives less than a star performance.

For the student of waterfalls the distinctive features of Scŵd Clungwyn Isaf can be traced to the presence of two parallel geological faults about 150 yards apart. Due to this, to the nature of the rocks exposed by the faults and to the tilt of the strata, the waterfall does not—as with Scŵd Gwladys and Scŵd yr Eira—fall at right angles to the river but, after descending in a curtain of water for approximately twenty feet over a steep ledge forming an acute angle to the river, then swings through an angle and falls another forty feet into the gorge to pursue its tumultuous passage through the ravine virtually parallel with the top part of the falls. With care and provided the river is low, it is possible to cross to the other bank of the river without returning to the footbridge, by wading along the river before it falls over the first ledge to form the first stage of the falls. The crossing is sometimes very narrow, and in places you are hardly more than a foot or two above the edge of the cliff of fall, but the view down the wild, heavily wooded gorge into the valley of the Mellte is unforgettable. Having made the initial crossing, you are safely on the wide glaciated 'pavement' of polished sandstone, over which you can walk to the eastern bank of the river. The alternative is to cross by the footbridge.

After Scŵd Isaf Clungwyn, the Mellte tumbles along a bed of shale which has enabled it to cut deeper into the sides of the ravine to produce a wider valley until once again the hard sandstone dominates and the river is restored to tumult as it roars through the narrow gorge between cliffs that are almost sheer.

Scŵd Isaf Clungwyn. After falling curtain-like over a ledge, the river gathers in a pool and swings round for its further descent.

Scŵd y Pannŵr (15)

(The Fuller's Waterfall)

At the end of the last century, in the course of a visit to the Vale of Neath, a member of the Cardiff Naturalist Society wrote of the densely wooded approaches to its galaxy of waterfalls that, 'The sky is fretted with intricate patterns of leafy twigs, and shapes of ash, oak, and hazel leaves are turned into transparent gold as the light filters through them.' The writer might have been describing especially the setting of the third major Mellte waterfall, which is known as Scŵd y Pannŵr, for in high summer, when the Mellte is low, the dense verdure of the crowding trees joins water, light and leaves in a spectacle of shimmering splendour.

The reason for the name of this waterfall, which is translated as 'the fuller's waterfall', is obscure, for this relatively inaccessible part of the river could never have been used for shrinking wool. The derivation is probably associated with the specially 'foamy' appearance of the fall and particularly the plunge pool, especially when it is in flood, when it resembles the traditional 'pandy' in action. The fuller used fuller's earth, a silicate, to absorb the pressed-out fleece grease, which shrank the cloth, and sprayed it with liquid soap, immersed it in water and then beat it between the fulling stocks for several days until the whole area of the pool was a sea of foamy suds. Wales had hundreds of riverside 'pandys'.

Pannŵr can be approached from two directions, from Scŵd yr Eira or from the Forestry Commission car-park at Porth yr Ogof (see page 63). At Scŵd yr Eira cross behind the falls and after walking about fifty yards down the right bank climb up a steep scree now marked at intervals with crude 'steps', which is the first stage of the journey to the Mellte. After the hard ascent, it is an enchanting walk with small, scattered groves of deciduous woodland and well-grown rowans, with magnificent views down the Mellte valley with the Brecon Beacons in the background. When you encounter the fenced Forestry plantation of conifers, follow the fence to the right, otherwise you will either reach the top of the high, inaccessible gorge or, descending along a path to the left, encounter the Hepste. After skirting the plantation, be guided by two successive noticeboards which direct you down a precipituous bank to the Pannŵr falls.

As with its neighbour Scŵd Isaf Clungwyn, the tilt of the rock strata at the point where Pannŵr occurs has resulted in the water flowing to one side of the valley so that, except when the river is in spate, the divided stream falls over the hard rocky protrusion in three graceful cascades. In flood the cascades join together in one surge of foam.

Scŵd y Pannŵr falls over a relatively small section of the sandstone ledge except when the river is full.

The Sychryd Waterfalls (6, 7)

(Waterfalls of the Dry Ford)

The River Sychryd has always tended to be the poor relation of the Vale of Neath waterfall rivers. Its waterfalls carry no names and have rarely featured in the 'Grand Tour' of the falls of the Vale. The valley itself is also difficult of access, and within a relatively short life the river is swallowed up by the voracious Mellte. Yet Sychryd is a waterfall river with many features of interest and well worth a visit.

Sychryd is formed from the unison of a number of small streams on the slopes of Hirwaun Common. It changes its direction of flow at least once, first flowing in a northerly and then changing to a west-north-westerly direction. Like the other rivers it has its moments of subterranean disappearance, when passing from Millstone Grit through Carboniferous limestone. In its last phases it flows along a deep, V-shaped ravine and produces two charming waterfalls before its final fall down a precipitous gorge, strewn with 'fault'-shattered boulders.

To reach the gorge waterfall of the Sychryd, continue straight through the village of Pont Nedd Fechan past a housing estate, to bear right over a very narrow bridge beneath which the Mellte flows in arboreal gloom. Park near the base of the big limestone cliff face of Craig y Dinas (the Fortress Rock) which rises almost sheer for 200 feet and is a site for Mountain Rescue practice. From here bear to the right, along the bank of the Sychryd between huge ivy-clad cliff walls. At the foot of the gorge is a famous limestone rock-fold known as Bwa Maen (the Bow Rock) from which stone was formerly sold for 'marble mantelpieces' at a price of 20 shillings per square foot in the early nineteenth century. Entrance to the gorge was formerly effected by a steel and wood ramp which after a long period of decay has been finally removed.

When Sychryd is high, it thunders down its narrow, precipitous gorge and effectively seals off access to the valley. If the river is in quiet mood, it is possible, but still with the greatest care, to make the wild-goat ascent of the gorge. Half-way up the gorge you pass on the left-hand side the pot-hole entrance to a cave which has been named 'Wills' Hole', the ingress point to an underground system (for experienced team cavers only). At the top of the gorge as you enter the valley is the abandoned silica mine where a vast roof conglomerate of rock is naturally supported by unquarried pillars of quartzite, miraculously free of 'joints'. Opposite the mine the river makes a delightful little pool from which the water flows over a sharp rock edge in a broad curtain of water. The Sychryd silica mine was once world famous. The Sychryd valley is indescribably lonely, and one has the sense of a lost world where Nature is slowly concealing the scars of men's despoliation of beauty and solitude.

The Sychryd pours down 'fault'-shattered rocks before its junction with the Mellte.

The Henrhyd Waterfall (18)

(Waterfall of the Old Ford)

To reach the Henrhyd Waterfall, turn off the Glynneath/Neath road at Onllwyn and then proceed to the village of Coelbren from which the site of a Roman camp, Y Garn, is discernible. The waterfall occurs in a densely wooded ravine cut through by the River Llech, a tributary of the Tawe. Geologists, for whom this gorge is of great interest, have advanced the theory that an 'ancestral' Llech once flowed in the opposite direction.

There are a number of minor waterfalls along the course of the River Llech, which is a left-bank tributary of the Tawe and has cut a deep ravine into the Coal Measures which lie on Millstone Grit. The glacial deepening of the Tawe Valley has forced the Llech to increase its down-cutting, in the course of which it has produced a number of small waterfalls. But the Henrhyd Waterfall, north of Coelbren village, is the best known and far and away the highest waterfall. It occurs outside the Vale of Neath proper and is accepted as a sort of sister falls to the Melincourt. Like that of the Melincourt, the Henrhyd gorge is a totally unexpected natural feature of great grandeur hidden in the midst of an industrial landscape. The densely wooded sides of the ravine are clothed with wych elm, ash, oak and lime with some hazel and birch and alder, and as in the Melincourt combe many rare mosses and liverworts thrive in the neighbourhood of the waterfall.

The River Llech falls about ninety feet over a vertical cliff on its way to join the River Tawe, at a point where the rock strata of the cliff are delineated with unusual precision. The lowest band is known as the basal grit and the upper level as the 'Farewell Rock', an intrusion of poetry into the realm of the geologist which derives from the fact that the 'Farewell Rock' was used to describe the sandstone rock underlying the last beds of clay ironstone and was also adopted by the South Wales miners who, when they encountered this fawn-grey, siliceous grit, knew that it meant the end of a coal deposit, a 'farewell to coal'. The thin layer of slaty coal above the 'Farewell Rock' stands out as a conspicuously black seam behind the falling water.

Since they were bequeathed to the National Trust, the approach and the descent to the glen have been made safe and easier to negotiate. The former descent involved a hard scramble down a steep path on the side of the ravine, from the east end of the village. Now there is a car-park and a carefully graded descent of steps. The way down is still steep, but older visitors can now negotiate it with the handrail support. The waterfall is intermittently visible through the trees as you descend, and suddenly it bursts into full view, two hundred yards away from the precipice of fall. The site of the waterfall in its steep, narrow gorge has been determined by the 'Henrhyd Fault', a fracture in the rock which crosses the stream at right angles.

The River Llech, a left-bank tributary of the Tawe, falls ninety feet over a virtually perpendicular cliff.

The Henrhyd is attractive even in drought. At low water the stream falls down the rocks in a slight, translucent skein, and when the river is almost dry the fall resembles nothing so much as a broad sunbeam.

The Henrhyd was the first waterfall to be visited by Michael Faraday in his enthusiastic tour of the waterfalls of the Neath Vale and its environs and, like the description of his visit to the Melincourt, his account of the Henrhyd Falls in his 'Commonplace Book' is filled with accurate and graphic detail under the heading of the 'Scŵd-y-Hen-rhyd or Glentaree':

The entry into the gorge was then a strenuous and even hazardous exercise for the thorns opposed our passage, the boughs dashed their drops in our faces and stones frequently slipped from our feet into the chasm below, in places where the view fell uninterrupted by the perpendicular sides of the precipices. By the time we had reached the bottom of the dingle our boots were completly soaked and so slippery that no reliance could be taken on steps taken in them. . . . We managed however, very well, and were more than amply rewarded by the beauty of the fall which now came into view. . . .

In his description of waterfalls—he also visited many other South Wales falls—Faraday's scientific discipline of dedicated observation is remarkably combined with that of the artist in words, and his closely observed description of the Henrhyd on a windy day is a particularly beautiful example of detailed observation:

The effect of the wind caused by the descent of the stream was very beautiful. The air carried down by the stream, the more forcibly in consequence of the minute division of the water, being resisted by the surface of the lake beneath, passed off in all directions from the fall, sweeping many of the descending drops with it. Between us and the fall the drops fell brilliant and steady till within a few inches of the bottom, when receiving a new impulse, they flow along horizontally, light and airy as snow. A mist of minute particles arose from the conflicting waters and being driven against the rocks by the wind cloathed them with moisture and created myriads of miniature cascades, which falling on the fragments beneath polished them to a state of extreme slipperiness.

Henrhyd in drought reveals the strata of the rocks with unusual clarity.

The Waterfalls of Mynydd Du (20, 25, 59)

(The Black Mountain)

When I think of the waterfalls of Mynydd Du, I have to separate this mountain range in my mind from the Black Mountains which lie principally between the rivers Usk and Wye in Monmouthshire and along the eastern border of Breconshire. The Black Mountain is sited in Carmarthenshire and the western borders of Breconshire, and its highest point is known as the Carmarthen Van (2,632 feet).

The Black Mountain is bordered by many rivers and a combination of boundary river valleys along its flanks, and the desolation of its high, boulder-strewn plateau gives it a distinctive topographical identity. The valleys and gorges, especially those of the rivers Haffes, Sawdde and Twrch, afford convenient avenues of access for the walker, though 'convenience' is perhaps something of a misnomer for the muscle-testing approach of the rivers Haffes and Twrch.

The Haffes rises below Llyn y Fan Fawr, one of the twin Black Mountain glacial lakes, and flows southwards along its gorge to join the Tawe, one of the most beautiful Black Mountain rivers, not far from the mansion of Craig-y-Nos, known for thirty years as the 'Home, Sweet Home' of the diva Adelina Patti. Access to the Haffes and to its waterfall is via a track leading through a farmyard opposite the Gwyn Arms in the scattered village of Glyntawe, on the Ystradgynlais road. The track runs north to the huge aggregates of glacial boulders and pebbles which make a veritable lunar landscape of the river bed. Except in flood you can cross to the other side of the river.

From here the course of the Haffes can, with difficulty, be walked along the bracken-strewn sidelands which run parallel above the bed of the river, but the preferred option is to take the track to the west which leads to the main plateau at about 1,600 feet and arrives in a roundabout way at the same eventual point above the river. This rendezvous of routes meets at Sgŵd Ddu (the Black Waterfall) where the Haffes falls seventy feet over a vertical cliff formed at a fault in the old Red Sandstone. It is a grotto of black rock where the sun penetrates only on days of high summer. The Haffes then tumbles down a rocky bed until it reaches the glacier-smooth boulders downstream where it is largely dissipated except in flood. Above Sgŵd Ddu the Haffes produces an impressive series of cascades as it flows along a 'glacial staircase' of rock from its source near Llyn y Fan Fawr.

The easiest approach to the other glacial lake, Llyn y Fan Fach, is along another Black Mountain river, the Sawdde, which one reaches via the little village of Llanddeusant sited near the end of a minor road from Henbont which is three miles south-east of Llangadog, just off the Llangadog/Brynamman road. Walk up to Llyn y Fan Fach, now a reservoir but which has lost none of its wild appeal, alongside the filter beds of the River Sawdde which comes down from the lake in slides and cascades. On

The Haffes river rises in the Black Mountain near the lake of Llyn y Fan Fawr and falls in cascades down rocky steps on its way to the Scŵd Ddu Waterfall.

the left, half-way to the lake, there is a small waterfall from an unnamed tributary. The lake shimmers darkly beneath the red, scalloped cliffs that plunge down from Bannau Sir Gaer popularly known as the Carmarthen van.

It is possible to reach Llyn y Fan Fach from the south-east through the valley of the River Twrch, which has the reputation of being the fiercest river in South Wales, so that when it charges in spate off the mountain—like the Mabinogion wild boar 'twrch' after which it is named—the river bed flints are rolled together with such force that they strike fire in the roaring darkness. Approach the Twrch valley from the village of Ystrad Owen, half-way between Ystalyfera and Brynamman. The immediate approach lane crosses the Twrch near the village, and from here the ascent of the valley is past ruined farmsteads, derelict mines and mills, over bracken-strewn sidelands where Welsh Black cattle can appear suddenly like heraldic beasts in the bracken oceans. The route goes high above the river, though the bank can be reached in a few places. It is a river of vivid pools and rapids, and there is one tributary waterfall half-way up the valley set in a veritable rock-garden colonized by an astonishing variety of plants. From the waterfall the route to the lake is across and up heavily bouldered contours, and about five miles from the falls a faint track leads to the top of Bannau Sir Gaer to provide a fine view of the lake and of the heavily wooded landscape to the north of the Usk reservoir. Also on the western edge of the Black Mountain there is another waterfall on a tributary of Nant Pedal river which rises at 1,500 feet in the Blaen Pedal marshes and flows southwards for three miles to join the River Aman half-way between Brynamman and Glanaman.

The eastern side of the Black Mountain is less visited by walkers, perhaps because it is wetter, with more areas of bog, but there are ephemeral rewards for the waterfall hunter. Along the eastern flank of Bannau Sir Gaer the River Tawe has carved a narrow ravine into which the Nant Tawe Fechan rushes in a series of cascades, while from 1,500 feet up the ridge an unnamed stream falls down the mountainside in a cataract to join the Tawe Fechan.

This is very rough country indeed, with dangerous swallets (deep depressions in the limestone areas where former surface streams have disappeared underground), in the boulder-strewn plateau, emphasizing the danger of sudden mists, and the need to carry a compass and to keep a weather eye on the sky. It remains surprisingly desolate and empty of people, lonely and unspoilt.

The River Haffes descends in the seventy-foot waterfall of Scŵd Ddu (The Black Waterfall) at the site of a fault in the Old Red Sandstone.

The Waterfalls of Nant Cwm Llwch (27, 28)

(Stream of the Lake Valley)

It is unlikely that the name of Nant Cwm Llwch, the Brecon Beacons stream formed from a welter of tiny tributaries and with an independent life hardly more than six miles duration, will strike a familiar note with many. But the dividends of spectacle which it yields to a day's energetic companionship place it high among mountain brooks.

Nant Cwm Llwch and its numerous tributaries are the principal falls-makers in the Brecon Beacons and rise in the lake of the same name under the towering hills of Pen y Fan (2,966 feet) and Corn Du (2,864 feet), the highest peaks in the Beacons. Formed during the Ice Age by the melting glaciers, the corrie lake Cwm Llwch lies at an altitude of 1,500 feet.

This oval mountain tarn, 130 yards long and 80 yards wide, is always dark and brooding (except on sunny days when white clouds above the peaks brighten the depths of the lake and the great precipice of Pen y Fan is reflected with marvellous precision) and has gathered apochryphal stories about its identity. Old guidebooks refer to it as a 'lake of unfathomable depth' and state that 'no bird ever flew near or swam upon it, nor will cattle or any other animal drink out of it'. A further depth comment reported that a one-time Recorder of Brecon 'failed to reach the bottom with two Llanfaes church bell-ropes tied together'. The truth is less dramatic, for at its deepest point the depth is eighteen feet. As with so many other Welsh lakes, that most ubiquitous of Celtic royal somnambulists King Arthur is reputed to be waiting nearby for the customary summons to 'save' Wales.

From this legendary moraine-impounded mountain tarn, Nant Cwm Llwch has carved an exit path about ten feet deep, through the humocky moraines, the grassed-over debris left by the glaciers. Almost immediately after its emergence, swollen by a welter of tiny streamlets and fed by a spring, the little mountain streams punctuate their singing descent down the mountainside with a series of white cascades along a sculptured Old Red Sandstone staircase of rock, with its 'treads' and 'risers' occurring over a descent of almost a thousand yards. This series of rock steps, due partly to differential rock resistance to erosion and partly to the action of the ice, is one of the unique white-water charms of the early life of the stream. After a sustained period of rain the whole mountainside seems to be transformed into charging white water.

The rocky staircase extends half a mile from the stream's lake exit, to a point marked by a grove of trees, a rare sight on these thin, rain-wind-scoured Brecon soils. This grove marks the site of the stream's first main waterfall, when Nant Cwm Llwch makes a double leap down a fault in the Old Red Sandstone. The trees that shroud and crowd over the waterfall are principally rowans, which blaze with red berries in the

In its descent the stream falls down a series of glacial steps of 'treads' and 'risers'.

clear air of the Beacons and are, above all other, the sylvan colonizers of waterfall environs. From this first waterfall the view downstream is superb, embracing on a clear day the Black Mountains, Mynydd Epynt and glimpses of Radnor Forest.

After its initial boisterous descent, the stream, after heavy rain, charges past Cwm Llwch Farm, now in use as a Youth Project Centre, and continues to roar towards Pont Rhyd Goch (Bridge of the Red Ford), a delightful little glen about three miles away. As the momentum of the mountain torrent slowly diminishes, it forms occasional deep pools and meanders through tree-dotted glades with Tennysonian chatter. At Pont Rhyd Goch it produces a number of cascades and waterfalls collectively known as the Rhyd Goch Falls. The main waterfall at Rhyd Goch is surrounded by a superb display of foxgloves, a blazing autumn pageant which may well have given its name to the 'Falls of the Red Ford'. Within a mile of Rhyd Goch the little stream joins the River Tarell, which enters the Usk at the Brecon suburb of Llanfaes.

The best approach to Nant Cwm Llwch is to cross the Usk by the main Brecon Bridge, and then turn left before the main Sennybridge road crosses the Tarell (opposite the Drover's Arms). Then strike a broadly south-westerly course along narrow lanes through the hamlet of Ffrwdgrech until the lane peters out at the disused military camp, map-marked 'The Login', near Cwm Llwch Farm. From this point the climb to the lake past the double waterfall follows a relatively well-marked track.

The route past the waterfall is associated with a pathetic happening at the beginning of the century. On the evening of 4 August 1901 little Tommy Jones, a miner's five-year-old son from Merthyr Tydfil, walking with his father to visit his grandfather at Cwm Llwch Farm, ran ahead with his cousin from the Login Military Camp. He then decided to return to his father but was never again seen alive. His remains were found after a month of searching on the ridge at a height of 2,250 feet.

The image of the little town-bred child, lost and terrified on the rough trackless mountain, climbing in the grim darkness past the thunder of the waterfall to a height of over 2,000 feet, before he fell to rise no more, caught the public's imagination and became a minor *cause célèbre* in the national Press. Later, an inscribed obelisk paid for by subscriptions was hauled by horse-sled onto the Beacons to the place where his pathetic remains were found.

The first waterfall produced by the stream in Cwm Llwch, which in summer is shrouded with scarlet-berried rowan trees.

The Waterfall Beast of Sawdde

Only once in the course of hundreds of miles of walking among the waterfalls of Wales have I encountered a river monster. It was a late September evening, the light almost gone and a milky mist rising in the valley. I was hastening back from Llyn y Fan Fach, the legendary lake which lies under the red crags of the Carmarthenshire van. Walking down the River Sawdde, now harnessed to carry water from the lake to the Llanelli township, I saw in the half-light a strange beast breasting its way up the white rapids of the river towards the lake. From perhaps fifty yards away it had the appearance of a huge aquatic rodent, possibly a member of the ichuemon family. The head appeared disproportionately large as it ascended the white water slide in its progress towards the lake.

Welsh legends of fabulous riverine denizens flashed through my mind. The most famous is that of the 'afange', the monster that was captured from the 'Beaver Pool' near Bettws-y-Coed. The story of its capture and disposal has lost nothing in the telling over the centuries. As early as the sixteenth century Camden, in his travel book *Britannia*, describes how the monster was taken from the pool, secured by heavy chains and dragged by a pair of oxen out of the district over the Snowdonia pass between Moel Siabod and Cribau. During the journey one of the oxen lost an eye, and the site of this is commemorated in the name 'Gwaun Llygad yr Ych' (Field of the Ox's Eye), while its tears formed a small lake which was named 'Pwll Llygad yr Ych' (the Pool of the Ox's Eye). The monster was deposited in Llyn y Ffynonlas.

The present returned and I realized that, apart from its large head, my crepuscular beast had more the appearance of a huge beaver, though the characteristic tail was not visible. In favour of this thesis, there was at least some degree of historical testimony for the former existence of the beaver on Welsh rivers, although it was apparently becoming rare even by the tenth century, when, for example in the laws of Hywel Dda (Hywel the Good), the skin of the beaver is given a scarcity value fifteen times that of the ox. Even so, centuries later beavers were reported as being busy on the Cardiganshire Teifi by Giraldus Cambrensis, and as late as the fourteenth century the poet Dafydd ap Gwilym wrote as though he himself had watched the beavers at work.

But alas, my expectation of encountering a fabled Welsh beast on the Carmarthenshire Sawdde vanished as I drew nearer. In the gathering twilight the monster turned out to be an astonishing piece of riparian topiary in which, after a period of torrential rain, the cascades had carved an uncanny likeness of a huge swimming rodent from the grassy verge of the river bank. The following day my monster had disappeared.

The legendary monster breasts the white water on its way to Llyn y Fan Fach.

Pwll-y-Wrach (29)

(The Witch's Pool)

The waterfall glen of Pwll-y-Wrach, a Site of Special Scientific Interest, is sited near Talgarth in the old county of Breconshire. It is difficult to imagine any reason for associating this waterfall woodland with a witch unless she were indeed from a very special coven, concerned with producing spells for the protection of a piece of unspoiled countryside.

The name Talgarth appropriately enough signifies 'the foot of the hill', and Talgarth lies under the long, dark escarpment of the Black Mountains, a favourite haunt of Francis Kilvert, the famous diarist. The River Enig, which flows through the glen, comes off the edge of the Black Mountains and enters the top, narrow section of Pwll-y-Wrach at a point about two miles above the waterfall, which occurs where an outcrop of hard rock (a concretionary limestone of exceptional hardness) has intruded into the Old Red Sandstone. At this point the River Enig is divided into two streams which form a pair of graceful cascades and provide a delightful focus for a walk up the glen.

To reach Pwll-y-Wrach, turn sharp right off the A479 from Abergavenny, as you enter Talgarth, and about half a mile past the town hospital the entrance to the Pwll-y-Wrach Waterfall is marked. The Pwll-y-Wrach glen is owned by the Brecknock Naturalists' Trust, and visitors must keep to the public footpath which runs the length of the reserve to the waterfall at the eastern end.

There are fine, tall oak trees with huge canopy crowns, interspersed with ash, birch, hawthorn, hazel and holly with the unusual addition of spindle and maple. This wealth of tree variety reflects the presence of the high lime cornstone in the rock profile. The spindle in particular has an interesting history, being an ancient craft tree whose close-grained yellow wood was used for making spindles, before the spinning-wheel was invented, and is still used in places for fashioning knitting-needles. The foliage of the other unusual tree, the field maple, makes a particularly fine autumn contribution to the golden foliage of the Pwll-y-Wrach glen. Near the waterfall the boulders and rocks, thanks to the high humidity associated with the spray, are richly endowed with mosses and liverworts, and there is a fine display of ferns.

In the woodland of Pwll-y-Wrach, there is a show of bluebells in season plus two varieties of wild orchid, dog's mercury, enchanter's nightshade and wild strawberry. In the open sections there are devil's bit scabious, betony and St John's wort. The floral spectrum includes heather, gorse, broom and dogwood. The influence of the high lime cornstone which has determined the scale and format of the waterfall has contributed uniquely to making Pwll-y-Wrach particularly rich in flowering lime-loving plants.

Pwll-y-Wrach, sited near the end of a delightful twenty-acre combe rich with trees and flowers.

Water-Break-Its-Neck (33)

The waterfall 'Water-Break-Its-Neck' is about a mile from New Radnor in Powys, off the A44 road to Builth Wells, where one turns right into a hidden turning opposite a sign marked 'Byway'. It is possible to drive along the lane, hardly more than a track, to within a hundred yards of the waterfall but usually, it is not difficult to find improvised parking; the walk along the lane to the waterfall goes between a towering hillside with occasional meadows and arable greencrops defying the bracken, and the lush flat meadowland of a big farm, surrounded by the swelling, smooth-topped vistas of the high Radnor Forest.

You are welcomed to the waterfall by a notice, 'Warren Woodland', where the unnamed tributary of the Summergil Brook which produces the falls, and which one has to wade to arrive at the waterfall, flows under a small bridge to its junction with the Summergil. The stream falls about eighty feet down a hard rock intrusion into a sunless amphitheatre overhung with dripping, heavily lichened trees and massed with ferns, where the white cascades of the waterfall are the brightest gleams in the gloom. The stream tumbles more or less vertically down the face of the cliff, and the surrounds are strewn with the trunks of fallen trees.

Water-Break-Its-Neck and the Warren Woodland were acquired by the Forestry Commission in 1951. The woodland has had a mixed history, being originally planted in 1870 and much of it felled during the Second World War. But as well as its own waterfall, it has other treasures, notably a number of magnificent trees to the north-eastern side of the falls. At a distance they look like cedars of Lebanon but they are in fact superb British examples of the great Californian redwoods popularly known in Britain as the *Wellingtonia (Sequoidendron gigantum)*, which can reach over a 150 feet.

On the adjoining land to Warren Woodland and the waterfall there is a Site of Special Scientific Interest. Radnor Forest is of course a 'forest' in the medieval sense of a huge tract of wild, uncultivated land often used for hunting. The SSSI comprises 2,078 acres including the highest hill in the forest, the Great Rhos (2,166 feet), of which over a thousand acres are above 2,000 feet. Here the Silurian shale is overlaid by a blanket of peat which supports a rich variety of plants, e.g. cotton grass, purple moor grass, numerous sedges, mosses and lichens. One tasty dividend of an early autumn visit to Water-Break-Its-Neck, to the Great Rhos and its neighbour Black-Mixen, is a feed of the bilberries with which Radnor Forest abounds. A much rarer delicacy is the cowberry, the delicious red version of the bilberry, which also supplements the pleasures of the waterfall.

The river falls into a dark grotto where the waterfall is the brightest gleam in the canopied gloom.

The Elan Valley Waterfalls (34–41)

The Elan valley reservoirs in Powys, which store Welsh water for export to Birmingham, are kept filled by the rivers Elan and Claerwen which provide the drainage for over seventy square miles of mountainous terrain rising to 2,115 feet. The average rainfall of the catchment area is seventy inches. The Ordnance map covering the area of the Elan Valley Scheme is notable for the number of waterfalls which are marked, though all are unnamed and half are on unnamed mountain streams. In addition, for those who wish to see falling water in an artificial context there are also, in wet weather, the 'synthetic Niagaras' of the overflowing reservoirs.

The Elan Valley Scheme, which by and large has been magnificently landscaped, comprises five reservoirs from which water is conveyed by gravity to the city of Birmingham, Caban Coch, Garreg Ddu, Pen-y-Garreg, Craig Goch and Claerwen, the latter by far the largest. Many of the waterfalls are sited in high, remote moorland and rough hill pastures overlying slates, grits and conglomerates of low intrinsic fertility where the Welsh Mountain ewe—stocked at about one per acre—can alone make a living. The number of cattle is in any case severely restricted on the Elan estate because of the danger of pollution.

The most easily reached Elan valley waterfall is, however, sited below the high gathering grounds and can be reached all the way by road. The Elan valley is approached from the town of Rhayader (a corruption of Rhaeadr) along the B4518 road, and the waterfall is reached by driving along the Caban Coch reservoir, then crossing the dam over the southern end of the Garreg Ddu reservoir, to reach a point half-way between Caban Goch and the southern end of the Claerwen reservoir. This unnamed waterfall is the most accessible of all the Elan valley falls, being sited a hundred yards fom the road in a large area of open moorland with numerous swallets and covered with heather and isolated clumps of gorse. Here the Claerwen river, after issuing from the reservoir, falls over a series of hard rock outcrops into a rocky channel set round with rowan trees. It is an 'amenity' waterfall with delightful picnic and rest facilities.

Most of the other Elan valley waterfalls offer a hard challenge in high, remote, wet countryside. Ffrwd Wen exemplifies this sort of search, which is only for those prepared for a hard, long walk. You can drive by car from the amenity falls on the Claerwen to the southern end of the Claerwen reservoir, where you should park because, although the track leads on for some miles, it is unsuitable for motors. Having walked to the end of the reservoir, strike off in a north-easterly direction across the high moorland, avoiding the boggy areas where you can without warning sink into your knees!

The most easily accessible waterfalls on the River Claerwen in the Elan Valley, where the occurrence of a geological fault has caused the rock to fall away in heaps of huge boulders.

Ffrwd Wen (the White Torrent) occurs on the River Nant Hirin not far from its source at the northern end of Lake Cerrig Llwydion Isaf (the Lower Lake of the Grey Stones). This is one of the most desolate areas of the high, rocky moorland which constitutes so much of the 45,000 acres gathering-ground which feeds the 2,000 acres of reservoir. The flocks of Welsh Mountain sheep which roam the barren peaty acres of nardus and molinia of the fifty-eight holdings or sheepwalks—many of the original holdings taken over are now derelict—are traditionally 'settled' flocks which are voluntarily 'tied' as the result of early close shepherding to their own unfenced stint of high land, so that, when the tenant retires, the 'settled' flock passes to the new occupant.

Ffrwd Wen provides a series of cascades and small waterfalls extending over a hundred yards of river. There are also two other collections of small waterfalls on a tributary of Nant Hirin close to the joining of the two streams. The return walk to the Claerwen reservoir from Ffrwd Wen is about fourteen miles, but there is a slightly shorter approach by taking the 'mountain road' leading from Rhayader to Cwm Ystwyth, in which you leave the B4518 near Llansantffraed Cwmdendon. On the way to Pont ar Elan, a small tributary of the Wye makes a series of cascades as it falls over a huge pile of glacial boulders on the slope of Craig Ddu. Park at Pont-ar-Elan, crossing a bridge over the Elan on the way to the confluence of Nant Hirin and the Elan.

There are also two minor waterfalls south of the Caban Coch reservoir. For these, park by a telephone kiosk at the southern end of Caban Coch, cross the Claerwen river, then turn right down a minor road which leads to the waterfalls near the junction of the River Rhiwnant and its Nant Pared tributary, in a channel of rock. There are fine views of the open country and the Caban Coch reservoir surmounted by its steep crags. The other waterfall is reached by turning left (instead of right) after the Claerwen bridge, to engage a mile-long track to the valley of the River Marchnant, when, after a steep climb along the river, you reach the waterfall near the thousand-foot contour.

To reach the waterfall marked on the eastern side of the Carreg Ddu reservoir, drive round Caban Coch and along the eastern side of Garreg Ddu reservoir. The waterfall occurs a few yards from the road where a tiny tributary falls over a rock to pass under the road into the reservoir. The falls on the western side of Garreg Ddu are reached by crossing the dam between Garreg Ddu and Caban Coch, parking near the little chapel which was built to replace the Nantgwillt chapel drowned by the scheme. Turn right along a wooded track, and after a short steep climb you reach the cascades in the wood on a stream which falls into Garreg Ddu.

The waterfall on the Nant-y-Sarn stream rises at a height of 1,400 feet on Moel Geurfon to join the Wye two miles north of Rhayader. Leave Rhayader on the Llangurig road to reach a telephone box after two miles, and park near a bridge over the River Wye.

Ffrwd Wen is sited in the remote, desolate country typical of the high catchment area of the Elan water scheme.

The Hafren Falls (45)

The Severn, known in its infancy by its baptismal Welsh name of Hafren, rises on Plynlimon at a height of over 2,000 feet in a peat bog between Carn Biga and Bryn Cras. Once it emerges from its amorphous origin, the little stream soon acquires identity and momentum, tumbling down a rocky bed, sometimes hardly more than a foot wide but boisterous and white-maned. When it enters the forest, it flows between the sombre magnificence of the conifers of Hafren Forest.

The Hafren stream enters the forest near the now almost vanished farmstead of Blaen Hafren, once the homestead of a large sheepfarm of several thousand acres of mountain. As a waterfall river, the Hafren confines its performance during these first few miles of life to numerous small cascades before putting on a distinctive and artistic waterfall performance near its forest entry where the widening stream is confined to a narrow passage hardly more than a yard wide. Having descended to form a pool, the river then makes a fan-shaped fall over a dome-shaped rock. The waterfall, though not large, is distinctive, rather like a giant wine bottle with a long neck and a wide, swelling body.

The best approach to the Blaen Hafren falls is to turn down Short Bridge Street from the Market Hall in Llanidloes and then left after the bridge over the Severn. Ignore the left fork half a mile further on, following the course of the infant Severn round to the right, keeping on the right-hand side of the river. After about two miles on a narrow road, enter the sprucewoods of the Hafren Forest, passing along the impressive wooded gorge to the left, into a parking and picnic place (with a small brick-walled hutment). This is the limit of car penetration. The shortest way to the Blaen Hafren falls from here is to walk to the first forestry road junction about a hundred yards from the park, then turn left through a gateway, after which the first right fork should be ignored and you continue walking straight ahead up the valley with the river below on your left for 1½ miles, until you come to a bridge over the river by a derelict homestead close to the falls. If you wish to walk up to the source of the Severn, follow the pathless ascent along the side of the stream from the waterfall.

Above the waterfall, sphagnum, green hair moss and many ferns thrive away from the river, and in season heather and gorse, the summer-flowering wild scabious, meadow sweet, marsh violet and bog asphodel.

Blaen Hafren is the main falls of the Severn stream but there are a number of small cascades inside the forest, all clearly marked on the forestry notice board.

The waterfall at Blaen Hafren resembles a bell or a bottle of 'Mateus Rosé' wine.

The Hengwm Waterfall (47)

It is tempting for the waterfall-hunter to attribute the possible derivation of the village name 'Forge', a tiny collection of cottages about 1½ miles south-east of Machynlleth, to 'fors', the Scandinavian word for waterfall. For Forge is the last village on the way to the waterfall of the River Hengwm which falls down a massive crag off the northern edge of Plynlimon. White water has always played a major role in the economic life of the Forge hinterland, where, together with quarrying, the production and weaving of wool were major industries. All the rivers carry numerous mention of the name 'pandy', the Welsh word for the wool-fulling pools which once existed in their hundreds along the mountain rivers and streams of Wales.

The road to the Hengwm falls runs broadly southwards from Forge, a narrow approach, which after about four miles reaches the farmhouse of Talybont Drain. Then proceed along a forestry road, crossing the Hengwm river at a ford, after which the road climbs rapidly, running more or less parallel to the Hengwm itself in the valley below. Then you reach a point above the river to catch the first sight of the waterfall, with directly ahead the huge grey crag down which the Hengwm slides and cataracts into the valley. From this point, to reach the foot of the falls, you have to force your way through a densely overgrown dingle and then through a plantation of infant conifers until you reach the river, a favourite fishing spot of herons.

When the river is full, the Hengwm covers the rock with white water. But the falls are singularly attractive too in drought when the river makes unusual arabesques in its descent along the scored granite. The fall faces due north and freezes most winters. Even in March the surface can be icy and extremely dangerous to negotiate, and Hengwm has several times chastised the recklessness of would-be climbers. The farmer from Talybont Drain told me that he had been forced on two occasions to call in a rescue helicopter to lift an injured climber off the rock.

The Hengwm Waterfall has long had a reputation for impassability. In 1402 the English King Henry IV failed to subdue the aspirations of Owen Glyndwr near Mynydd Bychan, which overlooks the Hengwm Waterfall. Here the English commander, determined to outflank the Welsh army, set his men to scale the waterfall rock. They failed and in the disarray of defeat by the roaring crag were routed by Glyndwr's men with great slaughter. For the Welsh, these craggy, thick-wooded fastnesses, with their steep-sided valleys, fast-flowing mountain streams, peat-bogs and falling water, had the classic advantages which accrue to defending patriots of all ages fighting in familiar country.

The Hengwm Waterfall in drought when the river 'draws' arabesques over the cliff of fall. The fall freezes every winter.

Ffrwd Fawr (48)

(The Great Stream)

In the old lead-mining areas of Wales the principal source of power was always water. The little village of Dylife on the edge of Plynlimon near Llyn Glaslyn was such a place where the precious mineral lodes and plenty of water to provide power co-existed. The area experienced intermittent zeniths of prosperous productivity, the period of greatest boom being from 1870 to 1880, when production reached 7,000 tons of lead ore a year. Prosperous mines meant prosperity for the farmers who found a ready market for their produce.

The agents of water-power were gigantic wheels, some of which reached sixty feet in diameter. Grouped round this union of water, ore and farming, the community of Dylife was a thriving one. A special railway was built to transport the Van mine ore to Caersws where the Welsh poet John Ceiriog Hughes was station master. But the story of mining often ends in dereliction, and Dylife today is set in the familiar lead-mining ambience of abandonment, desolation and environmental ravage.

The word Dylife signifies 'a place of torrents', and this aspect anyhow has not changed, for near the village the waterfall Ffrwd Fawr still makes the same awesome plunge of over 200 feet down its vertical precipice of fall. To find the falls, pass through the village of Staylittle towards Pennant along the B4518, turning left about two miles from the former, where Dylife is signposted. The road climbs steeply, flanked by the edge of the Plynlimon escarpment, while to the north-west there is a particularly fine panoramic view across the Dovey valley to Cader Idris, the Taren range and Aran Fawddy.

Near the first layby parking place on the right and a hundred yards off the road, the Twymyn river, which at this point is only just over two miles from its source, falls over a near vertical cliff of hard sandstone into the dark chasm below. The waterfall is one of the highest virtually unbroken descents of water in Wales. After the waterfall, the stream flows hundreds of feet into the deep gorge, one of the most impressive in Wales, until it eventually begins to widen out as it approaches the hamlet of Pennant. In the creation of this gigantic canyon the River Twymyn was assisted over the aeons by the actions of glaciers and a series of crustal faults and the differential erosion resulting from mixed geological strata of shales, grits and sandstones.

Ffrwd Fawr is meant to be viewed from the road but about a hundred yards from the fall the fence into the land leading down to the edge of the gorge has been flattened by those who have been determined to make a closer inspection. Intending closer viewers should be warned that, especially after rain, the approach can be as slippery as glass, and they should keep well away from the edge of the giant gorge.

Ffrwd Fawr formed by the River Twymyn near the village of Dylife, the 'Place of Floods'.

Pistyll y Llyn (49, 50)
(Waterfall of the Lake)

For the waterfall-hunter, the Angler's Retreat is the source of one of Wales' famous cataracts which has its origins in the lake called Llyn Pen-Rhaeadr (Lake at the Head of the Waterfall). For the angler it is the famous site of a remote fishing lodge serving four lakes, the New Pool, Llyn Conach, Llyn Dwfn and Llyn Pen-Rhaeadr. The area is one of boggy marshland, lonely and remote, on the northern edge of the Plynlimon range, rich with moorland flowers where the molinia turns golden in the autumn and runs and bows before the winds off Plynlimon. The skies are haunted by crying curlew and hovering raptors, the trout lakes a gathering-ground for flights of autumn mallard.

The Anglers' Retreat can be reached either by the mountain road from Talybont or from the A44 which goes from Llangurig towards Aberystwyth, turning right at the old lead-mining village of Ponterwyd, just before the bridge over the River Rheidol. This takes you towards the Nant-y-Moch reservoir and continues towards Talybont. Two miles from the reservoir's northern end, a stony road to the right is signposted (faintly) 'Angler's Retreat', and a looping, climbing forestry road leads to the New Pool.

Llyn Pen-Rhaeadr lies to the north of the fisherman's lodge and is the source of the River Llyfnant. In early progression after its exit from the lake, the infant Llyfnant flows in little sallies and gullies through shale and mudstone, its course lit with small cascades, bright with ferns and flowers. But it does not stay long in its upland home, for less than half a mile from the Llyn Pen-Rhaeadr source it flows round a rocky bend and without warning disappears over a blind precipice into the valley below. From this point of descent there is a magnificent panoramic view of half of Wales.

The Llyfnant falls 300 feet over a precipice in which the slate strata have been pushed into a sharp anticline by movements in the earth's crust. Except after heavy rain the falling stream divides during its descent into a number of white skeins until a point near the base of the rock face, when they join again in foamy unity. After torrential rain there is an almost unbroken fall and a subsidiary waterfall on the left-hand side. Ferns and flowers on the path of descent grow almost into the falls itself, and clumps of heather and small rowans have taken root in clefts and fissures.

The rocks over which Llyfnant falls and flows are in places as polished and slippery as glass, and to descend from the Angler's Retreat by the side of the cataract demands both experience and great care. On the eastern slope nearest the falling water, erosion has marked the hill with big bands of eroded slaty shale. More than most waterfalls—all of which demand care and prudence—Pistyll y Llyn should be treated with respect, for it has claimed a number of victims in recent years (including one Member of Parliament).

Pistyll y Llyn: on the eastern slope nearest the cataract, erosion has marked the hill with big bands of eroded slaty shale.

The usual approach to the waterfall, however, is via the base of the falls. For this, turn off the Machynlleth/Aberystwyth road to Gelli Goch, proceeding to the hamlet of Glasbwll, which you leave on the right, driving for about a mile until a T-junction marks the nearest point to the falls where cars may be parked. At nearby Cwm Rhaeadr Farm the right-of-way skirts the farm buildings until it reaches the track which leads to the falls about a mile and a half away, across the moors, past a fenced-off derelict lead-mining shaft.

After its precipitous descent as Pistyll y Llyn, the Llyfnant pursues a more leisurely winding course through flat, marshy moorland with frequent shallows and high gravelly points with small twin waterfalls near Cwm-Rhaeadr farm. The river then moves into a densely afforested narrowing vale which becomes progressively more precipitous as it approaches Glasbwll. Here the dark array of planted conifers almost shuts out the sky, and the gigantic walls of trees in the narrowing confines of the valley are more than a little claustrophobic. Glasbwll is today mostly a hamlet of peace, where the loudest sound is the babble of the river (with the occasional noise of trees being felled), but it was formerly the rural hub of a hinterland alive with local industries, the fulling of cloth, tree-felling, preparation and provision of oak logs for the New World and the stripping of oak bark for the local tanneries.

From this historic hamlet, the Llyfnant now turns sharply west, its course along its final miles to the Dovey estuary dominated by the geological 'Llyfnant fault', and the course of the river is now once again reminiscent in miniature of the tumultuous cataract of Llyn Pen-Rhaeadr. The course of the Llyfnant until it joins the Dovey estuary is particularly beautiful. But the road along the river to the T-junction with the Aberystwyth/Machynlleth road is not one for the timid motorist. The approaches carry no warning at either end, though for much of the way it is hardly wider than one car, with virtually no passing-places and with steep drops to the river. With a wide ribbon of grass growing down the centre, it is essentially a walker's road.

Preparing to roar: the Llyfnant about to descend from its upland home into the valley in the form of the Pistyll y Llyn cataract.

The Tanat Waterfall (55, 56)

The River Tanat rises at a height of just under 2,000 feet in the Berwyn Mountains to the south-east of Lake Bala and to the north of Lake Vyrnwy. Quite early in its life, it falls several hundred feet down Craig Wen into the Cwm Pennant valley in a cataract visible for miles.

To reach the Pennant valley, go to the old lead-mining centre of Llanfynog on the B4391, and turn left onto an unclassified road immediately after crossing the Tanat Bridge. An extremely narrow road with few passing-places takes you to the village of Pennant Melangell, where the valley of the Tanat widens into green meadows under the foothills of the Berwyns. The road peters out across a cattle-grid into a farm lane which ends at the holding where you can park with the farmer's permission. The track to the waterfall leads past the farm barn where you have to wade a shallow tributary of the Tanat. The valley opens out again as you approach the cataract, with the boggy approach criss-crossed with numerous tributary becks from the hills.

The Tanat belongs to the Berwyn Mountains which, with their smooth, swelling contours and rolling heathery plateaux, are surprisingly rich in waterfalls. None is more memorable than this high cataract, and autumn is perhaps the best season to visit it, not merely because the river is more likely to be full and the cataract in full cry but because the Berwyns are in their prime, the flanks of the mountains and the surrounds of the cataract aglow with bracken; at the foot of the falls large, vivid patches of flowering gorse flare among the heavily lichened boulders.

A day out should certainly include a picnic by the foot of the falls followed by a scramble up the Berwyns above Cwm Pennant. The visit should end on the way home at the tiny eighth-century church of Pennant Melangell, which carries a charming legend. One day, when the Prince of Powys was hunting, his hounds flushed a hare which raced into the undergrowth in an attempt to escape. Here the Prince found a young woman in prayer, protecting the hare under the fold of her garments. The hounds refused to take their prey, and the virgin, whose name was Monacella, told the Prince she had lived there for fifteen years, to escape an abhorred marriage, arranged by her Irish king father. Greatly moved, the Prince gave her the land to found a sisterhood of mercy. Her effigy can be seen in the church, with two hares peeping out from her waist.

There is white falling water of grandeur comparable to the Tanat cataract in an adjacent valley to the south where the River Goch falls as Pistyll Gyfyng down the massive rocks of Tap-y-Gigfran (the Tap of the Raven). To reach Pistyll Gyfyng, turn left just before the bridge at Llanfynog. The final approach is for walkers only, with deep drops from the approach track to the valley below, where the river joins the Tanat.

Early in its life the River Tanat falls several hundred feet over Craig Wen in the Cwm Pennant valley.

Pistyll Rhaeadr (57)

(The Spout Waterfall)

The village of Llanrhaeadr-ym-Mochnant (Church by the Falls of the Swift Brook) is sited about six miles from the little town of Llanfyllin in the old county of Montgomeryshire. It derives its modern fame from its proximity to the highest waterfall in Wales, Pistyll Rhaeadr, which is well signposted from the village. Its church is famous as the sixteenth-century benefice of the Reverend William Morgan, who translated the Bible into Welsh, published in 1588, which rescued and reshaped the Welsh language. Morgan worked on his translation in a summerhouse in the rectory garden to the sound of running water.

Wales' highest waterfall belongs to the Berwyn Mountains, which are renowned for their waterfall splendour. Pistyll Rhaeadr—the name is something of a tautology for both words signify a waterfall—is formed by the River Disgynfa which rises not far from the Berwyn lake of Llyn Caws (the Lake of Cheese), so named from its resemblance to the shape of a Welsh cheese. After its mile of mountainside course from above the lake, the river has to plunge 240 feet over an erosion-resistant sandstone precipice. The Distgynfa makes its fall in two great leaps. The first near-vertical torrent of water is 'broken' eighty feet from the base by a small band of rock, fronted by a natural arch through which the river then pours in a mass of white foam, for its final descent to the deep plunge pool at the base, which has a white shingly shore. The waterfall itself is contained inside a chasm of towering black rock, topped with conifers and surrounded by fine woodland beech and oak, larch, ash and sycamore trees, many of them planted over a century ago. The nearby rowans are magnificent.

After its dramatic fall the river flows under the small footbridge which enables one to cross to the other bank of the river and scramble up the slaty screes to a point above the falls. (The bridge also provides an ideal vantage-point from which to enjoy the spectacle for those who like their viewing made easy.) The Distgynfa then hurries to its junction with the Nant-y-Llyn river, and after their confluence the two streams become the River Rhaeadr to flow through lush, tree-fringed meadows—still flanked part of the way by screes and high banks—until it joins the Tanat river below Llanrhaeadr-ym-Mochnant.

George Borrow described the waterfall in glowing terms in his *Wild Wales*: 'There are many remarkable cataracts in Britain and the neighbouring Isles. But this Rhaeadr, the grand cataract of North Wales, exceeds them all. I never saw water falling so gracefully, so much like beautiful threads as here.' At the falls Borrow was regaled by a farmer's wife with a cup of foaming buttermilk, and as he drank she told him that the waterfall was sometimes very dreadful: '. . . especially in winter; for it is then like a sea, and roars like thunder or a mad bull'.

Pistyll Rhaeadr, Wales' highest sheer-drop waterfall, descends in two leaps, passing through a natural outlet of rock on the way.

The Cenarth Falls (61)

The village of Cenarth, whose centre was historically accepted as the meeting-place of the old counties of Carmarthen, Pembroke and Cardigan, is on the bank of the River Teifi, six miles south-east of Cardigan. The big expanse of roaring white water in the centre of the village, where the river is crossed by a seventeenth-century twin-arched bridge, is collectively known as the Cenarth Falls. They cover about two acres of the river which comes storming down the heavily wooded Teifi gorge, through rocky gullies, over big 'table rocks', dashing and smashing against black mid-stream boulders and rocky islets, turning the whole area into a sea of foam.

Cenarth is surrounded by medium-sized upland farms, and the river for centuries was the principal pre-shearing washing-place where, in Dryden's words, the farmers could 'steep in wholesome waterfalls the woolly sheep'. There is a tradition that below the bridge, where the river is reduced to a calmer pace, though still quite fast running, the rocks along the river bank have been polished and worn by the passage of countless flocks of sheep down the centuries. The site is a flock-washing 'natural' because there is enough current to make the sheep strike out strongly to ensure a penetrative fleece-wash, ample space to accommodate a large flock and a take-off point which demands a flying leap, shepherd-assisted in the case of yearlings having their first wash but more philosophically taken by the older ewes who have been there before.

The sheep at Cenarth were swum across twice just below the waterfalls, and the use of the deep, free-running river was made possible by the employment of Teifi coracle fishermen as mid-stream shepherds—their work was traditionally a useful summer source of income before the sewin began to run strongly, but in the past five years a change to unwashed shearing has been made, which has interrupted the centuries-old custom below the Cenarth falls. But the whiteness of the fleece remains an economic factor, and 'as white as the Cenarth falls' is still the ultimate local accolade for a winning fleece.

The Teifi is one of only three rivers in Wales—the other two are the Tywi and the Taf—where the coracle is still allowed to fish for salmon and sewin (the Welsh name for salmon-trout), though only just. For over the years a battle has raged between the anglers and the 'netters', who include the coracle men, with fewer and fewer coracle licences being issued. Cenarth coracle fishermen work in pairs at night, with a net stretched between the two craft being dragged along the bed of the river to seek the salmon or sewin going upstream to spawn. The Cenarth coracle has changed hardly at all in a thousand years except that, instead of the original cowhide, the modern version uses calico made strong and watertight by layers of hot tar or pitch. Coracles are

The old mill by the Cenarth Falls where the 'undershot wheel' is again being powered by the river.

A5

incredibly light, a full-sized craft weighing about 20 lb, and they are marvellously manœuvrable.

While Cenarth coracle fishing has declined, another activity by the side of the waterfall has been revived and has increased the attraction of a visit to the falls. Just over a quarter of a century ago the stone mill that has been slapped with waterfall spray for over two centuries began to produce again the uniquely delicious smell of Welsh oatmeal. The moss-green waterwheel was repaired, virtually rebuilt, the gears recogged with ash, the complex system of chutes, hoists and augers brought back to life, an exercise in skills performed by ageing tradesmen. The pen-stocks of the millpond were brought into working order, the leet was cleaned out and the roar and clatter of the water-mill were added again to the sound of the falls.

The flavour of Welsh oatmeal is different from that of the Scottish. The cleaned oats are placed on perforated aluminium sheeting above the old coke-fired kiln—at Cenarth the kiln was rescued from the pile of old mill equipment—and cooked slowly for upwards of four hours until the berries lose half their weight. Left overnight to cool, they are then lightly touched by the millstones to loosen the outer husk for winnowing, after which the oats are returned to the stones for fine grinding. The oatmeal is then hand-sieved, and the so-called 'second husk' is fed back to the millstones to be made into Welsh sucan (flummery). Once again, after a hiatus of years the old mill, obedient to the lonely 'clacking' wheel, wafted a delicious quintessence of oatmeal nuttiness over the white water.

Today the old mill is also concentrating on wholemeal bread, ground from organically grown wheat between the ancient millstones which contribute their own flavour to the wholemeal flavour of the wheat. For those interested in the design, the Cenarth waterfall mill is driven by an 'undershot wheel' and has 'paddles' and 'floats' as opposed to the usual 'buckets', so that the water falls on to the bottom of the wheel and drives it *backwards*.

'White as the Cenarth Falls' was the supreme accolade for the sheep fleeces produced by the neighbouring farms. The sheep were washed below the falls and shepherded by coracles.

The Mynydd Mallaen Waterfalls (62, 63, 64)

The little town of Cilycwm, in the old county of Carmarthenshire, is 3½ miles north of Llandovery in the upper part of the Tywi valley. The road to Cilycwm out of Llandovery crosses the Tywi on its way into the hills. Cilycwm is a gateway into a delightful and still largely unspoiled region, and within four miles of the town one can visit three waterfalls, all falling off the rough, lonely heights of Mynydd Mallaen.

Leave Cilycwm along the road marked to Lake Brianne, the huge new reservoir at the headwaters of the River Tywi. Half a mile from Cilycwm turn left down the farm lane to Glangwenlais and seek permission to visit the farm waterfall on the River Merchon. A small bridge over the river leads from the farmyard: proceed along the bank in a north-westerly direction through scrub woodlands and boggy upland dingles to the confluence of the rivers Merchon and Gwenlas, after which the moorland opens out and you follow the right-hand river bank to the waterfall.

After rising near Esgair Ferchon at 1,423 feet, the Merchon flows through rough country for a mile and then falls over a crag of volcanic rock. The rocky site of the falls has been carved into a series of extraordinary shapes by the elements, including one long tongue of petrified lava sculpted in the likeness of some huge Silurian reptile crawling down the hills. The waterfall itself is not unduly impressive but the walk is through lonely country, and the rocks surrounding the falls are worth a visit for themselves alone.

To visit the next in the triad of Mallaen waterfalls, return to the Cilycwm/Lake Brianne road, and it is almost immediately visible a mile from the road, falling down a 300-foot gully, broken by crags and boulders. It is formed by a mountain stream, Nant Rhosan, which rises 1,100 feet up, near the crag of the same name on Mynydd Mallaen, and falls obliquely into the meadow at the foot of the falls. This is very much a 'farm waterfall' with no way of approach except through the farmyard, which has no public footpath. On the day of my visit, when I approached the farmhouse, I had the delightful experience of being welcomed by numerous Welsh collies with collie pups of all sizes.

The third waterfall is deep in a Forestry Commission plantation. Turn left along the Cilycwm/Lake Brianne road. After coming out of the farm road to the second waterfall, take the second turning to the left, proceeding as far as the marked entrance to the Cwm-y-Rhaiadr plantation, where you should park. After a walk of about a mile and a half along the forest road, the waterfall appears, tumbling for several hundred feet down a steep gully. The first hundred feet are hidden by trees, but it is possible to clamber up the gully to a point above the trees, where you can watch Nant Rhaiadr bouncing from crag to crag. All three waterfall rivers flow into the Tywi.

Three miles from the little town of Cilycwm, in a wild and remote valley, the Merchon stream falls over weird volcanic rocks.

The Hafod Waterfalls (68, 69)

It is logical to visit the Hafod waterfalls after a visit to the gorge of the Devil's Bridge, not merely because of their proximity but because in a past age the Rheidol Gorge was part of the estate owned by the proprietor of Hafod.

Thomas Johnes inherited the Hafod estate in 1783 and determined to turn this beautiful corner of Cardiganshire, with its rivers and waterfalls, its mountains and valleys, into an earthly Paradise. On the site of the old house which was demolished, he built a magnificent Gothic-style mansion, laid out gardens, grottoes and riverside walks, and built bridges, a school and a church, all regardless of cost. He reclaimed hundreds of acres of land, poured vast wealth into improving the lot of the impoverished peasantry, then sunk into a semi-barbarous way of life and planted many millions of trees. The record of his achievements, his no less magnificent failures, the prodigality of his altruism, and the final bankruptcy of his fortunes as well as his dreams, is history.

Hafod is owned by the Forestry Commission, and nothing now remains of its former splendour except a rather special waterfall to testify to Johnes' dream. It is unique of its kind and is known as 'the Waterfall of the Robber's Cave'. It was an object of admiration to the flow of visitors two centuries ago, and it remains equally a cynosure of admiration today.

To reach the Robber's Cave, about two miles from the site of the old mansion, now a caravan park, take the B4574 road from Devil's Bridge towards Cwm Ystwyth, passing the Ministry of Agriculture Experimental Farm, to arrive eventually at the church of Eglwys Newydd (built by Thomas Johnes, burned down in 1932 and now beautifully restored). You can park here and then proceed down the nearby forestry road, to go left at the second turning, crossing a concrete bridge over the Ystwyth, until after about a mile, within sight of Dologau Farm, you strike sharp right up through the forestry plantation. The track later swings left towards Nant Gau river, a tributary of the Ystwyth, and continues along and above the river until it reaches a series of high rocks blocking further access up river.

Here there is the roar of falling water, but there is apparently no waterfall. One clambers down to the river to search out the source of the roar only to be faced again with a blank wall of rocks. The key to the mystery lies in an aperture in the slaty rock face above the end of the path, through which one enters a tunnel in the rock, just high enough to walk upright. The roar grows louder until, after a bend to the left in the forty-foot-long tunnel in the rock, the waterfall appears, falling over a precipice of rocks at the entrance of the cave. The effect is singularly beautiful, with the rock of the cave aperture outlining the white curtain of water like a black picture-frame. You are

Through the aperture of the Robber's Cave the hidden waterfall of the Nant Gau is suddenly visible framed by the rock of the cave.

assaulted by a cold, moisture-laden current of air and, when the river is high, by showers of spume and spray which can soak you in seconds. The scene was graphically described in 1776 by amateur artist and author George Cumberland, who published a little volume entitled *An attempt to describe Hafod*. Nothing seems to have changed in the time since he followed roughly the same path as today, to the Robber's Cave.

> The ravine now narrows fast . . . when a small, close, cave is perceived on the right; on entering which a roaring sound of water assaults the ear which increases on advancing through the dark passage; when turning suddenly to the left, light breaks in and you see through a large aperture, a luminous sheet of water, falling just before you, with noisy velocity, into a deep hole beneath. After rains this aperture cannot easily be approached, as the spray beats in like a mist and sometimes even the torrent, but the contrast of the gloomy passage you are in, with the light of the opening and the rapid motion of the waters, hanging down before it like a shower of icicles, produces an effect on the mind that is very imposing . . .

There seems little doubt that the cave which allows one to see the falls was excavated by Cwm Ystwyth miners, to many of whom Thomas Johnes gave life-saving employment when the lead- and silver-mines were failing. According to a contemporary acquatint by John 'Warwick' Smith, who takes some obvious poetic licence in portraying the scene, the cave was then served by stone steps, and there was a tree-trunk bridge to the other bank of the river. Presumably the stories about the cave being a hiding-place for smuggled goods and footpads' loot arose in later years.

While the Robber's Cave is the showpiece of the Hafod waterfalls, there are a number of others. Two hundred yards from the cave a stream falls and slides 150 feet into the river, and there are a number of other small waterfalls created by the river along its rocky bed. There is also a small waterfall, Rhaeadr Peiran, formed on the river of that name as it falls down a wooded defible about half a mile from its junction with the Ystwyth. In the Hafod heyday selected waterfalls were illuminated at night with 'Bengal Fire' (a particularly brilliant light produced from black sulphide of antimony traditionally used as a shipwreck signal) which was burned to floodlight the magnificent gardens and grottoes of the Hafod estate.

The poet Geoffrey Grigson has developed the idea that Hafod which was probably passed through by Coleridge after his visit to the Devil's Bridge gorge, provided some of the inspiration for *Kubla Khan*. It is an interesting thesis. All the ingredients of *Kubla Khan* were to be found at Hafod, particularly if one adds from the Devil's Bridge gorge, which Coleridge visited, 'the deep romantic chasm' and the waterfall of the Mynach, where 'huge fragments vaulted like rebounding hail'.

A tributary of the Nant Gau falls into the river a hundred yards from the cave.

The Mynach Waterfall (70)

For many miles the little River Mynach flows without arrogance through the hilly countryside to the north of Devil's Bridge until it enters the great chasm where the River Rheidol waits to receive it hundreds of feet below on the floor of the gorge. The Mynach's descent is due to its being a hanging valley, high above the Rheidol, its bed exempted from the glaciation, fault and down-cutting which have deepened the main ravine. At its point of entry into the gorge the Mynach has carved a deep, narrow gully through the rock which is crossed by the famous Devil's Bridge, a three-storey conglomerate of bridges. The first and lowest bridge is credited to the Cistercian monks of the now ruined abbey of nearby Strata Florida, and this bridge can be dated with precision because it was crossed in 1188 by the historian Giraldus Cambrensis, in his Welsh tour, seeking Welsh volunteers for the Crusades. The middle bridge was superimposed on the monks' bridge in 1708, and the topmost unit was added at the beginning of this century.

The Mynach effects its final entry into the Rheidol gorge with a series of waterfalls from a height of approximately 400 feet, the last falls being the longest and highest. The spectacle can change rapidly from thin skeins of white water to a monolithic sheet, when torrential rain falls into the catchment area above the gorge.

The gorge has been well laid out for the safety and convenience of the viewer, and although there is a turnstile entry, the layout has effected minimal intrusion into the elemental wildness and drama of the scene. One of the best vantage-points from which to view the entire drop of the Mynach is a platform just before the 91-step 'Jacob's ladder' which leads down to the footbridge over the Mynach near the base of its waterfalls. As you begin the ascent up the other side of the gorge, there is a fine close-up viewing-point for the first Mynach cascades about a hundred feet below the road bridge, where the water has excavated a deep plunge pool, using whirled rocks and stones, the stones themselves worn smooth by the action of the water. This viewing-point is near a secret Aladdin's Cave, once used as a hiding-place, to store their ill-gotten gains, by the 'Children of Matthew', medieval footpads who terrorized the area until they were taken, and the two brothers hanged and the sister burned.

George Borrow visited the gorge in 1854 and stayed at the Hafod Hotel. He was particularly impressed with the last phase of the Mynach falls: 'You view it from a kind of den to which the last flight of steps, the ruggedest and most dangerous of all has brought you. Your position here is a wild one. The fall which is split into two is thundering beside you, the basin or cauldron is boiling frightfully below you, hirsute [*sic*] rocks are frowning terribly above you and above them, forest trees, dank and wet with spray and mist are distilling drops and showers from their branches.'

From its hanging valley the River Mynach falls 400 feet down the Devil's Bridge gorge to join the River Rheidol at the bottom of the ravine. On the right is the entrance to the brigand's cave.

The Rheidol Waterfalls (71–74)

The River Rheidol has two main claims to fame. It is the principal creator of the Devil's Bridge gorge, and it is one of Wales' fastest-flowing rivers, falling 1,750 feet in its 28-mile course from its Plynlimon origins in the lake, Llygad Rheidol (the Eye of Rheidol), to the sea. Compared to the millennia of its zenith power, the Rheidol of today has been much depleted by the plunder of its waters for the hydro-electric dam at Nant-y-Moch and the lower barrage near the village of Ponterwyd. Even so, it is still, along sections of its course, a creature of cataracts and cauldrons.

Rheidol can be seen for about a mile each side of Parson's Bridge, which is reached along a tortuous but signposted and handrailed descent from the church of Ysbyty Cynfyn. The Parson's Bridge, now replaced by a modern structure, was formerly used by visiting parsons who tied up their horses at the bridge when visiting to conduct services at the Ysbyty Cynfyn church. Quite close to the bridge, a few hundred yards up the steep western ascent, there is a delightful 'hanging valley' waterfall which can be seen falling hundreds of feet through the densely wooded slopes of the eastern bank to join the river below. But the true measure of Rheidol's former power is the Devil's Bridge gorge, where movements of the earth's crust have also contributed to the immense down-cutting of the river, as well as river-capture (page 7).

Rheidol erupts into the gorge in the form of the Gyfarllwyd waterfall, which tumbles down a declivity of hard rock in a series of falls and cascades. The Gyfarllwyd is barely accessible, though a few hardy anglers have been known to make the hazardous descent from an encampment about 500 yards on the left beyond the Hafod Hotel along the Ponterwyd road. There is a view of the falls, set in its vista of woodland from a point inside the gorge before the main step-down descent to the gorge floor begins.

The depletion of the Rheidol also means that the Devil's Bridge gorge is now subject to minimal further down-cutting from the river, for at least half the river's flow is diverted through pipes to the generating station below Devil's Bridge.

On its exit from the gorge, now also carrying the waters of the Mynach, the Rheidol flows quietly for most of its final course to the sea, except that, on the northern side of the valley about three miles from its point of exit from the gorge, a waterfall from the high tributary Nant Bwa Drain descends from its 'hanging valley' to join the Rheidol. Then, encountering a last obstacle of hard rock across its course, the Rheidol produces one final fall (there is a salmon-pass as well) which provides a swansong of falling water before the river flows home to the sea.

The Rheidol falls which have a 'pass' for migrating salmon are sited near Capel Bangor. The Rheidol is one of the stormiest of Welsh rivers.

The Ceiriog Waterfalls (76)

To find the waterfalls of the River Ceiriog, you take the turning marked Glynceiriog at the southern end of the village of Chirk (just above the road sign which welcomes you to Wales), almost opposite the Hand Hotel. Your destination is the village of Llanarmon Dyffryn Ceiriog about ten miles away, and with the Ceiriog river flowing towards Chirk as your accompanying companion, you pass through the old quarrying village of Llansanffraid Glynceiriog, usually shortened to Glyn, the stone-built village of Pandy, sited in a bend of the river and the former riverside site of a major wool-fulling industry, and the hamlet of Treceiriog with its little wayside church, to arrive after ten delightful miles at Llanarmon Dyffryn Ceiriog, the highest village on the river, at the foot of Rhos Mountain (1,887 feet).

The Ceiriog rises at the northern end of the Berwyns, on the moors above Corwen, and when it reaches Llanarmon it is about six miles from its birthplace. To reach the Ceiriog waterfalls from the centre of the village, turn right down a lane faintly sign-posted Swch-cae-rhiw. It is a narrow lane with few passing-places, and the Ceiriog runs alongside a few yards away on the right. Apart from the extreme narrowness one's progress is slowed by the scores of tame pheasants which are raised for annual slaughter by a local rearing syndicate; they insist on running in front of the car, so that it takes bouts of prolific horn-blowing to lift them over the hedgerows. Four farmsteads are passed on the way but the most interesting landmark is a tiny, isolated chapel at the hamlet of Pentre. Wales has many of these minute places of worship built to serve the remote hill farms where lonely lives could be warmed by worship and the meeting of kindred souls. A mile from the chapel the Swch-cae-rhiw farmhouse appears on the right; it is corrugated-fronted with the blistered paint now giving it the appearance of stonework from a hundred yards away. Here you can park near a little bridge which crosses the boisterous Berwyn tributary, Nant Rhydwilwyn, which joins the Ceiriog nearby.

If you decide to seek the waterfalls by walking upstream (with farm permission if there is anyone in), pass through a field gateway, down a steep paddock to the bank of the river where you can walk and wade upstream to the first waterfall. It is not the easiest of walks because in places you have to get round protruding cliffs and rocky bluffs, which involves wading through the cold white water. The first fall is reached after about a mile, at a point where the river has to fall over an outcrop of sandstone rock, which has resisted the down-cutting of the mountain stream. It is a lonely waterfall, in this respect somewhat similar to Scŵd Einion Gam in the Vale of Neath, though one is hemmed in here not by a narrow limestone gorge but (on the east side) by the rounded foothills of the Berwyns, rising over a thousand feet up from the river,

The first waterfall on the River Ceiriog immortalized for Welsh poetry-lovers by John Ceiriog Hughes.

carpeted with bracken on the lower slopes and with heather and molinia on the rolling summit. The waterfall crag presents a formidable obstacle to further progress upstream except for climbers, so one either has to return downstream or make a breath-taking scramble up the western scree to the gloriously solitary bracken plateau high above the river. From here you can enjoy a magnificent panorama of the great Berwyn crescent with a distant perspective of two other waterfalls with which the stream punctuates its descent from its high moorland source.

Walking by the River Ceiriog, most Welshmen will remember John Ceiriog Hughes, the nineteenth-century poet who passed his childhood roaming the Ceiriog valley. What Tennyson's poem 'The Brook' has been and is to succeeding generations of English poetry-lovers, John Ceiriog Hughes' much-anthologized 'Mountain Stream', 'pure, pellucid, wandering through the vale, singing in the rushes', is to readers of Welsh poetry. The poet would find little changed today in the lovely valley of his Ceiriog stream. The waterfalls are unaltered, the upper pair tinged with the colour of brown peat as they roar down the rockfaces into miniature canyons; the giant oceans of bracken still possess the sidelands that soar above the falls, the dwarf willows and the struggling alders bow and bend to the wind, the rowan still hangs its berried branches over the white water, and, all around, the mighty moorland crescent of the mountains broods.

Ceiriog was a true romantic who spent his last years as station-master of a tiny station at the village of Caersws where the industrialist and philanthropist David Davies of Llandinam had built a six-mile railway, to bring out the lead ore from the Van lead-mines at Dyliffe. In the intervals between the few trains a day Ceiriog passed his time writing poetry. He is not one of the great Welsh poets in the mould of Dafydd ap Gwilym. He tended to write too much and concentrate his content too little. But the short lyrics which are standard inclusions in all Welsh anthologies have stood the test of time, and the words run through the minds of those with a knowledge of Welsh who come to admire the Ceiriog waterfalls and the mountains which are associated with his name.

'Ceiriog Country', where the River Ceiriog has cut ravines and produces a series of waterfalls.

The Diserth Waterfall (78)

There is a senior American Senator from Wyoming who is said to seek his night's rest to the sound of falling water—it is not specified if it is from his own estate or a 'tape', perhaps of one of the great falls in the Wyoming Yellowstone National Park. It is certainly not given to many to have private falls but there are some Welsh villages where the village waterfall is a fringe benefit for those who live there. One such is the village of Diserth sited 2½ miles from Rhuddlan, in Clwyd, and mentioned in the Domesday Book of 1083 as possessing a church, with its own priest, and a cornmill.

It is fitting that Diserth should have its own waterfall, for it is surrounded by powerful, never-failing springs on the limestone uplands above the village. The Ffyddion, the river which produces the falls, has its source in Ffynon Asa (Asaph's Well) and flows down the slopes of Bryn-y-Felin until it reaches the village, when it falls sixty feet over the cliff. The waterfall is associated with a fault—part of the Vale of Clwyd Fault—which has given the river erosive access to the softer middle strata of shale. The top bed of strongly jointed hard limestone has also tended to break away along the bedding planes, and these boulders can be seen along the bed of the stream. Earlier photographs of the falls show a 'picture-book' waterfall with untramelled surroundings, but there is now a small charge for viewing.

Like most waterfall rivers near inhabited areas, the River Ffyddion has been harnessed as a workhorse over the centuries. The gradient from the high source ensured a fast-flowing stream with the all-important watermill attribute of reliability, because the powerful spring of St Asaph's renders it more or less independent of rainfall fluctuations. Local studies by Prestatyn High School have established that in the eighteenth century the Ffyddion and its waterfall provided the power for ten mills. These were mainly for the preparation of corn grist and bread flour, but one was in use for the production of cotton.

The well of St Asaph was formerly second in flow only to the great well of St Winefride at Holywell, with an estimated output of seven million gallons a day. It is also said to have had a reputation for healing and sanctity in the Middle Ages.

More than any other area in North Wales, the Diserth hinterland is limestone country, the water heavily impregnated with lime, the upland surrounds dotted with saucer-shaped depressions (swallets) marking the ingress points of former surface streams which have sunk underground through the joints of the limestone: the sort of country which the poet Auden celebrated in his famous poem 'In Praise of Limestone'.

The Diserth Waterfall fed from 'Asaph's Well' which had a reputation for healing in the Middle Ages.

The Dolgoch Waterfalls (79)

The tiny village of Dolgoch is approached from the B4405 off the Dolgellau/Tywyn road. Proceed along the B4405 from Tywyn for three miles through the valley of the River Fathew. The public road bears left near Dolgoch, where you leave it for a large car-park near the entrance to the Dolgoch waterfall ravine, bequeathed in 1902 by a local benefactor, Robert Jones-Roberts, as a public recreation ground. In 1977 extensive work was executed in making the waterfall and woodlands safely accessible to the public, widening the paths, building new stairways of approach and erecting handrails.

The waterfalls are produced by the River Dolgoch, falling from a high hanging tributary valley into the deep main valley of the Fathew. The Dolgoch falls are unusual in that they occur, as it were, in two storeys. The first and principal waterfall is seen immediately one enters the ravine along the Dolgoch stream. It falls in a curling curtain of water down a tree-shrouded rock, richly colonized with mosses and ferns, the fall being broken a third of the way down by a rocky protuberance which gives the fine cascade an oblique angle of fall. The river then gathers into a pool before continuing its journey down the boulder-strewn bed to the entrance of the ravine. From the viewing-place one can ascend to the site of the other two falls, which come down through the trees in high, thin skeins of water.

The Dolgoch Waterfall ravine forms part of the Tal-y-Llyn valley in which the two principal rivers are the Dysynni and the Fathew. The Dysynni flows out of Tal-y-Llyn lake along the line of the Bala/Tal-y-Llyn Fault but having flowed south-west for two miles makes an astonishing right-angled turn west of the village of Abergynolwyn before turning back to its south-westerly course towards the sea at Tywyn. The reason for this change of course to the sea remains a matter of conjecture. The Fathew also rises south of Abergynolwyn and runs along the line of the fault before joining the Dysynni about a mile from the sea. Both valleys have been deepened by glaciers but it is a curious anomaly that, of the tributaries that join the Fathew, none produces waterfalls comparable to the Dolgoch when it falls into the Fathew ravine.

While these falls are the highlights of the ravine, Dolgoch has another claim to fame in having given its name to the Dolgoch Falls Station on the little narrow-gauge Talyllyn railway which travels from Tywyn to Pendre, Rhydyronen and Bryngias, prior to crossing the three-arched viaduct over the Dolgoch ravine into Dolgoch Falls Station, where, tree foliage permitting, passengers are able to enjoy the waterfalls of the wooded gorge. There are two more stations, Abergynolwyn and Nant Gwennol (the terminus).

The main Dolgoch Waterfall drops from its hanging valley into the vale of the Fathew, near the entrance to the coombe.

The Cader Idris Waterfalls (80)

Of the eight routes to the summit of Cader Idris, (2,927 feet), the approach from the south near the village of Minffordd is one of the hardest but also the most rewarding. For upwards of half a mile of steep scrambling one is regaled by the spectacle and sound of cascades and waterfalls as the mountain stream makes its tumble into the Tal-y-llyn valley below.

To reach the approach to the Cader Idris waterfalls, proceed to Minffordd eight miles from Dolgellau on the Dolgellau/Machynleth road and then turn onto the road marked to Tywyn, the starting-point of the Talyllyn railway. A few hundred yards from this turning-point there is a double iron gate by the roadside—appropriately manufactured by 'Idris & Co'. From here walk across a small stream past the private residence formerly known as Llwyn-dol-Ithel, past masses of rhododendrons and avenues of planted trees and shrubs to reach the boulder- and-stone-strewn steps of the waterfall-flanked ascent.

The torrents of Nant Cader which fall through the Cader Idris Nature Reserve are the product of the stream's descent from a hanging valley into the drainage below. In the course of its descent it produces all the permutations of falling water, slides, vertical falls, plunge pools, water-meets and miniature cataracts, sometimes hidden behind shrubs and foliage and in places falling down eroded 'staircases' of rock. The waterfall environs of the Nature Reserve ascent are rich in plant life, because of the abundance of running water, interspersed with ledges of rock which have retained pockets of good soil containing base minerals and also lime in a form available to the plants. On the way up to the plateau leading to Llyn Cau, botanists have recorded lady's mantle, green spleenwort, harebell, ox-eye daisy, beautiful St John's wort, wood sorrel, bitter vetch, aspen, primrose, mossy saxifrage, rock stone crop, wild angelica, devil's scabious, lesser meadow rue and others. A short distance away from the cascades and waterfalls the woodland slopes grow a considerable diversity of trees and seedlings in their dank glooms, ash, aspen, mountain ash, hazel, holly, bramble and hawthorn. Again the key to the richness of arboreal species is the occurrence of pockets of good soil among the rock ledges and high points of the precipitous slopes.

One of the best rest and picnic spots of the ascent is near the initial plunge point of Nant Cader before the cwm opens out into the wide approach to the summit. From this point one has the best of both the Cader Idris worlds, the companionship of the waterfalls as well as the panorama of the multi-coloured volcanic walls to the north. From here one can follow Nant Cader along the wide, stony plateau as it threads its way between the huge mountain walls of the southern Cwm from Llyn Cau. In this

The source of the Nant Cader, whose waterfalls make the Minffordd ascent to Cader Idris so memorable.

cwm, gouged by the glacier into the southern slopes of the ridge, Llyn Cau gleams in its setting of volcanic escarpments which hem it in on three sides. It was the subject of Richard Wilson's most famous Welsh painting in the mid-eighteenth century, now in the Tate Gallery.

To savour the full splendour of the Llyn Cau scene as well as that of the other cwm lakes on the northern side of the range, you can make a hard, vertiginous climb to the west of the lake between Craig Cwm Amarch and the summit of Pen-y-Gader. This affords a wonderful view of the companion cwms, the hollowing-out of which has left the hanging sharp ridge which is a principal feature of the range with its long miles of precipice. The dramatic fall-away of the long south-east ridge, Cwmrhwyddfor, is due to one of the most dramatic geological land movements in Wales, known as the Bala/Tal-y-Llyn Fault (this fault is responsible for both the Bala Lake and that of Tal-y-Llyn.)

Anyone resting by the side of Llyn Cau after the hard scramble past the waterfalls and the walk across the plateau cannot fail to understand how this great mountain, its brooding lake and corrie have become the site of many legends. There is a legendary monster in the lake, and a myth that anyone who sleeps in the cwm will wake blind, mad or a poet. And who was the eponymous, mysterious Idris - giant, king, Welsh prince, perhaps even Arthur himself? There is a consensus that the word 'Cader', which is the Welsh for 'chair' is meant to signify 'seat' as in 'seat of learning'.

Cader Idris is not even among the five highest mountains in Wales but it is one of the most loved, and the spectacular climb past the Nant Cader waterfalls is a worthy prelude to the magnificence of the scene which unfolds.

Down from hanging valley, Nant Cader tumbles almost a thousand feet to its confluence with the River Fawnog below.

The Arthog Falls (82)

Few Welsh villages are as perfectly poised between the mountains and the sea as the little village of Arthog on the southern shore of the River Mawddach estuary, about three miles from Barmouth. Like many Welsh villages, it was at one time closely associated with large quarrying operations just outside the village, housing the quarry workers in the neat terraced houses which still remain. With its easy access to the beaches of the Mawddach estuary, Arthog makes some pretension to being a small resort. But it is its position close below the Cader Idris range that gives it its special appeal and has made it so well known, especially for its waterfalls.

The stream which produces the falls is named the Arthog and has its small beginnings in tiny Llyn Cyri, which is fed by rain and springs 1,200 feet up in a small corrie one mile east of the Braich Ddu ridge of Cader Idris. The stream flows fast down its little rocky channel for the first part of its course and begins to form its waterfalls on the wooded slopes about half a mile from the village, falling in cascades for over a hundred yards, passing eventually into the grounds of Arthog Hall, a castellated residence with magnificently wooded surrounds.

There are a number of approaches to the Arthog waterfalls, the most direct being via a public foot path almost opposite the village church where you leave the road to climb a steep flight of steps, leading to a narrow track above the stream as it flows through the grounds of Tyn-y-Coed. After about half a mile the track reaches a bridge across the stream at the point where it falls down a face of rock in a series of waterfalls and cascades before charging under the bridge, increasing its down-cutting in the steepening, narrow ravine. This little bridge is the best vantage-point for a view of the Arthog falls.

The same way to the falls can also take one up to two beautiful lakes on the Cader Idris spurs. The twin Cregennen lakes are about 800 feet above sea-level, notable for their deep blue colour and fringed round with conifers hemmed in by mountain walls. The energetic walker, after climbing to Llynau Cregennen, can make for the western section of the Cader Idris Bridge. The path climbs with a relatively easy gradient to Tyrau Mawr (Big Towers), whose summit is 2,167 feet above sea-level.

The space between Arthog and the sand of the Mawddach estuary is a mixture of marshland and meadow marked by two little knolls called Fegla Fach and Fegla Fawr. There is a toll footbridge across the estuary from near Fegla Fawr and of course the famous railway bridge to Barmouth across the estuary also passes it. So Arthog has, as it were, the best of many worlds—the enchanting estuary of the Mawddach (the favourite North Wales river of John Ruskin and Gerald Manley Hopkins), a fine waterfall fed from a Cader Idris corrie lake, and a series of superb walks.

The Arthog Waterfalls formed by the River Arthog which flows down from its source in tiny Llyn Cyri, below the Cader range.

Pistyll Gwyn (84)

(The White Waterfall)

On a fine day, free of its frequent misty haze, the peak of Aran Benllyn (2,901 feet) dominates the view across Lake Bala from the town end. This is many people's first view of the Arans which run southwards from the lake to the little village of Dinas Mawddy just off the main road from Welshpool to Dolgellau.

The approach to Pistyll Gwyn is via the little village of Llanymawddy. You can reach the village either by turning off the Welshpool/Dolgellau road towards Dinas Mawddy (Llanymawddy is a few miles beyond) or from Bala, passing through Llanuwchllyn, a village delightfully sited in the low-lying strip of country formed by three Bala Lake tributaries, the Twrch, Lliw and Dyfrdwy (Dee). Out of Llanuwchllyn one turns right onto the narrow road from Llanuwchllyn to Dinas Mawddy, down the notorious Bwlch y Groes which, at 1,790 feet, is the highest pass in Wales (with one rather hair-raising 200-yard section of 1 in 4 gradient). Before the descent, along narrowing lanes, one is regaled with views into the heart of the Arans, dominated by the twin craggy peaks of Aran Benllyn and Aran Fawddy (2,970 feet), seen across moorland and meadow through tree-shaded field gateways.

At Llanymawddy the turning-point to Pistyll Gwyn is by the side of the Baptist chapel and leads up a steep track onto open moorland through which the River Pumryd flows. Follow the river bank for about two miles to a vast pile of scattered glacial boulders leading to the rocky defile which is the final approach to Pistyll Gwyn. The Arans here are very hard walking country for the heathery and grass ridge summits are littered with grey granite boulders—like the plateau of the Black Mountain in Carmarthenshire. The River Pumryd slides and falls 500 feet over a massive precipitous crag, then down the valley over a rock bed, before joining the River Dyfi.

A traveller familiar with the Arans can find his way from Pistyll Gwyn to Aran Fawddy, but it is a rough, unmarked route demanding great care. The easier approach is from Aber Cywarch about four miles south of Llanymawddy, a tiny granite hamlet built on the bank of the turbulent Cywarch stream at the bottom of the beautiful Cywarch valley. A road negotiable by cars turns right in the village near a waterfall where sewin jump on their way upstream, continuing towards Bryn Sion and Tyn-y-Twll, after which the road ends. Marshy valley fields follow the course of the spumy Cywarch stream, and then the sheep-track along the Hengwm can be followed towards the ridge that goes from Drysgol from where the blue Craiglyn Dyfi lake is visible, to Drws Bach, which takes you on the final hard climb to the summit, which is surmounted by a modern cairn. You can return the same way or, a longer, more fatiguing option, return via Pistyll Gwyn to the village of Llanymawddy, one of the cleanest Welsh villages, whose cottages glow and shine in the clear mountain air.

Pistyll Gwyn, where the River Pumryd falls over a steep crag in a wild fastness in the Arans.

Rhaeadr Ddu (86)

(The Black Waterfall)

This Rhaeadr Ddu Waterfall is sited inside the official Nature Reserve of Coed Ganllwyd above the village of Ganllwyd about five miles north of Dolgellau. The Reserve which is leased by the Nature Conservancy from the National Trust, lies between 200 and 450 feet above sea-level, on the western flank of the River Mawddach. The waterfall occurs on the River Gamlan which rises at just over a thousand feet in a tiny corrie lake. The Gamlan flows with increasing pace down its ravine, making a picturesque small waterfall well worth visiting about a quarter of a mile before it encounters a large outcrop of hard rocks to produce its second, main waterfall of Rhaeadr Ddu, after which the river continues its gorge down-cutting until it joins the Mawddach, itself swollen by the capture of the River Eden, near Ganllwyd. The Gamlan has the reputation of being one of the clearest and purest of Welsh mountain streams, because it flows over such a hard rocky bed.

Rhaeadr Ddu is unique among Welsh waterfalls in having a beautiful carved slate tablet facing it on the northern bank of the Gamlan stream. It is a romantic story, a worthy celebration and tribute to the wild beauty of the historic falls and the Gamlan glen which have drawn enthusiastic visitors for almost two hundred years. (In particular, Thomas Love Peacock has left us many accounts of his visits to Rhaeadr Ddu) (page 28).

It was during the latter half of the nineteenth century that an angular rock protruding from the ground opposite the waterfall was found to have a heavily weather-worn inscription carved on its surface. The inscription defeated the attempts of local antiquaries to decipher it (though some of the words were known to be in Latin) and produced some weird interpretations. The mystery was solved by Eggerton Phillimare, who, in a 1919 copy of the antiquarian *Bygones*, revealed the lines to be from Thomas Gray's Latin 'Alcaic Ode written at the Grande Chartreuse' in 1740 when the poet was travelling on the Continent with his friend Horace Walpole. The original carving on the rock opposite Rhaeadr Ddu is almost gone but with imaginative zeal the National Trust has had the relevant verse of the poem, together with a side-by-side English translation, reproduced on a magnificent tablet of slate and placed by the original. The tablet reads as follows:

> ON THE FACE OF THE ADJOINING ROCK, IN THE LATE 18TH CENTURY, LINES FROM THE ALCAIC ODE BY THOMAS GRAY
>
> WERE CUT BY AN UNKNOWN HAND. THE INSCRIPTION WAS IN LATIN. HERE ACCOMPANIED BY AN ENGLISH TRANSLATION.

Rhaeadr Ddu in the Ganllwyd glen, one of the best-loved waterfalls in North Wales.

'O, thou! the Spirit 'mid these scenes abiding,
Whate'er the name by which thy power be known
(Truly no mean divinity presiding
These native streams, these ancient forests own
And here on pathless rock or mountain height
Amid the torrent's ever-echoing roar,
The headlong cliff, the wood's eternal night,
We feel the Godhead's aweful presence more
Than if resplendent neath the cedar beam,
By Phidias wrought, his golden image rose),
If meet the homage of thy vot'ry seem
Grant to my youth—my wearied youth—repose.'

The poet of the 'Elegy Written in a Country Churchyard' was a fervent lover of waterfalls, and the poem in the glen was probably carved by William Alexander Maddocks (1774–1828), who built the embankment across Traeth Mawr and in so doing reclaimed thousands of acres of land from the sea as far as the pass of Aberglaslyn, or by one of his poetry-loving guests at his residence nearby. He was visited at Dolmelynllyn by Shelley as a long-staying guest, and by many other poets, and he both encouraged and facilitated public visitation and enjoyment of the beauty of Rhaeadr Ddu, which was on his estate. His love of this part of Wales sustained him through a life beset with some grim vicissitudes.

This waterfall glen of fifty-nine acres is today a Nature Reserve of particular interest to the botanist because the continual spray from Rhaeadr Ddu and the rushing descent of the river through the Reserve, coupled with an eighty-inch annual rainfall and the dense canopy of dripping trees, have given rise to an extremely high humidity. As a result the rocks in the gorge are luxuriantly carpeted with an abundance of mosses and liverworts which include some extremely rare species, and there is also a fine display of rare ferns. The floor of the boulder-strewn woods away from the margins of the river is dominated by bracken (and bramble). But it is the variety of trees which gives this waterfall glen its particular interest. The dominant tree is the oak, both the sessile (the acorns of the sessile oak are distinctively stalkless) and pedunculate varieties, which are currently from fifty to eighty feet high. Along the banks of the river, the oak mingles with some fine ash, whose crowns share the woodland sky. Test borings carried out by the Forestry Commission have shown these trees to be from 100 to 130 years old. This splendid variegation of glen woodland is enhanced by some fine birch, wych elm, beech, rowan, cherry and European larch, and groupings of sycamore.

Apart from the National Trust the other official body involved in the care of the glen is the North Wales Region of the Nature Conservancy Council at Bangor, which is as jealously protective as is consistent with public access.

Close to Rhaeadr Ddu a beautifully carved slate tablet inscribed with Thomas Gray's 'Alcaic Ode' has been sited by the National Trust.

Rhaeadr Mawddach (89)

(The Mawddach Waterfall)

The story of Welsh gold and its association with the marriages of British royalty is shot through with the name of a North Wales river and its waterfall. The river is the Mawddach, the waterfall Rhaeadr Mawddach.

The Mawddach has its source in a high marshland area known as Waun y Griafolen (the Moor of the Rowan) a few miles west of Bala Lake, 600 feet above sea-level, and flows to its Cardigan Bay home at Barmouth after a journey of just over twenty miles. It is broadly paralleled for some of its course by the River Gain, which it eventually swallows just before the twin waterfalls—one on each river—which occur at a geological fault point in the forest of Coed-y-Brenin. Like the river and the waterfall the forest through which the Mawddach flows also has royal overtones, for its former name—Vaughan Forest—was changed in 1935 to 'Coed-y-Brenin' ('Forest of the King') to commemorate the Silver Jubilee of King George and Queen Mary. It is one of the oldest Forestry Commission forests in North Wales.

To reach Rhaeadr Mawddach cross Pont Dolgefeilan near the village of Ganllwyd on the Dollgellau/Trawsfynydd road. The entrance into Coed-y-Brenin is well marked, and in the early stages of the three-mile walk to the falls the River Eden, which comes in from the north-west, accompanies you for part of the way in pastoral tranquillity through meadows dotted with sheep and white-faced cattle. The sideland to the river is heavily afforested, and given one's reservations about the dead march of conifers on the Welsh hills, the stands of 'noble fir' are certainly impressive when their towering glooms are lit by the slanting beams of the setting sun. But on the left of the road upstream to the falls the sidelands have remained virtually unafforested, colonized and lit with gorse and broom, wild flowers and self-regenerated deciduous trees.

Rhaeadr Mawddach occurs at a point just before the river has its confluence with the Gain. As perhaps befits a workhorse exploited for its strength, the Rhaeadr Mawddach is a broad, low falls but discharging a big volume of water into its plunge pool. For almost a hundred years, according to whether the mine was active or temporarily closed down, it was the principal source of power for the Gwynfynydd gold-mine. The waterfall was harnessed direct to a huge waterwheel of sixty-foot diameter, then later piped direct to the turbine. Gwynfynydd, in its first year of operation in 1864, yielded gold then valued at £35,000. The magic lure of the precious metal drew men from far and wide, and among those who came to seek adventure, if not fortune, at Gwynfynydd in the 1930s was the young Patrick Hastings (the future famous forensic chemist) who, before disillusionment set in, was in charge of the gold-processing furnace at the Mawddach mine.

To process the richest Welsh ore, the ore with the so-called 'visible gold', Rhaeadr

Intermittently for over a century, Rhaeadr Mawddach provided power for the processing machinery at the Gwynfynydd gold-mine.

Mawddach provided power for a stone-crusher which broke up the gold-bearing rock or 'gangue'. The crushed gangue was then transferred into 'Britten Pans' where it was marinated into terminal slurry, with a continuous flow of water from the Mawddach. The gold-bearing slurry was then mixed with mercury and later drained into small leather bags, when as much as possible of the mercury was squeezed out. The remainder was processed in the furnace retort. The gold was stored in a strong room behind a door specially brought from the closed Dolgellau gaol.

Some of the riverside equipment which had specific application to Mawddach gold processing has been rescued and restored and is on display at the Visitors Centre thanks to Prince Charles, who expressed strong interest in its conservation after a visit. There are still a number of stone walls and ruins remaining by the Mawddach, and part of the large-diameter cast-iron pipe which carried the water from the falls to the turbines is still in position. The mines closed in the 1970s, though from time to time industrialist entrepreneurs still seek to revive the search for Welsh gold.

Little now moves near the white water of Rhaeadr Mawddach, where hundreds of men once toiled and the romantics dreamed of fortune from Mawddach gold. It is the haunt of kingfishers, pied flycatchers, dippers, wagtails, the solitary herons that fish the deep-coloured pools and the large numbers of knapsacked humans walking the legendary forest. The legends survive despite the intruding screech of power saws felling the timber, from among the 16,000 commercially managed acres. The forest still has its old-established herd of fallow deer, which also has its own legendary association. Long ago a holy hermit who lived in the forest suffered a misfortune, when his only working ox was killed by a falling tree, so that he could no longer plough and cultivate for his simple food. So the wild deer came down from the hills and hitched themselves to the plough, and as they turned the sod, the wolves followed peacefully behind, dragging the harrows over the upturned furrows to prepare the land for the holy man's sowing.

The water was carried by pipe direct to the turbine or to a huge waterwheel over fifty feet in diameter.

Pistyll Cain (88)
(The Cain Waterfall)

In one sense the Napoleonic Wars, by sealing off the Continental Grand Tour, an established feature of the upper-class life style and culture in the eighteenth century, helped to bring a number of Welsh waterfalls into prominence. In South Wales the waterfalls of the Vale of Neath and its environs became 'standard' beauty spots to be visited, painted, written about and eulogized. In North Wales, apart from Cader Idris, Snowdon and the Vale of Conway, the trio of waterfalls Rhaeadr Ddu, near Dolgellau, Rhaeadr Mawddach and Pistyll Cain, a few miles away, became indispensable features in the Celtic Grand Tour equivalent.

The River Gain—the name is linguistically mutated into Pistyll Cain—rises in high marshy country about five miles from the River Mawddach source in the cotton grass moorlands not far from the black heights of Dduallt. The River Gain flows more or less due south and after a few miles joins the River Mawddach where the Mawddach makes a more or less right-angled turn southwards. From this point the Gain takes the name of the Mawddach, though in the versified opinion of a local bard it is the River Gain that actually 'drowns' the Mawddach, even though it loses its name in the process.

The junction of the two rivers is made memorable by the twin waterfalls which are found near the confluence as though the two rivers were each concerned to show their paces in a final trial of strength before the fusion of waters. Rhaeadr Mawddach is the more powerful, broad and powerful like a shire cart-horse, the former workhorse of the old Merioneth mine of Gwynfynydd. Pistyll Cain, about fifty yards away in a more or less straight line, is more elegant, three times as high, falling in a graceful descent a hundred feet or more into a hidden grotto, richly endowed with trees and shrubs and flowering plants. After its descent the Gain flows to its junction with the Mawddach under a Bailey bridge which is a convenient spot to enjoy the spectacle of the waterfall.

Pistyll Cain's tiny dell of descent is a singularly memorable setting, densely wooded with oak, ash and rowan. There are also clumps of rhododendron to add colour in season and numerous flowering plants, including St John's wort, water avens, golden saxifrage and a wealth of ferns and mosses which thrive in the spray of the falls. When for a brief period during the days of high summer the sun is able to penetrate the canopy of foliage, the grotto is transfigured into a jewelled alcove of green and gold. Pistyll Cain falls with almost aristocratic elegance when the river is low, though this grace is rapidly engulfed in a roaring storm of white water when the river is high. It is not difficult to credit Pistyll Cain with human 'one-upmanship' in preceding its immolation in the Mawddach with this attractive performance in sylvan surroundings.

A few yards from Mawddach the River Gain makes a fine waterfall in its own little combe fronted by a 'Bailey bridge'.

Rhaeadr Ddu (92)

(The Black Waterfall)

If you were to enquire about the whereabouts of Rhaeadr Ddu at the little village of Maentwrog, three miles from Ffestiniog, you would certainly be directed to the waterfall on the River Prysor. At the village of Ganllwyd twenty miles away you would with equal certainty be directed to a waterfall of the same name, sited in the Nature Reserve of Coed Ganllwyd, where the River Gamlan charges into the Reserve off the slopes of the Rhinog range. There are three 'Black Waterfalls' in Wales.

The Prysor flows out of Llyn Conglog-mawr near Foel Cynfal and, having made a westward U-turn through Cwm Prysor, flows west into Trawsfynydd lake. The man-made lake at Trawsfynydd dates from 1926 and was formed as a source of power for the generation of electricity at the hydro-electric station at Ivy Bridge, near Maentwrog. Now it provides the coolant water for the Trawsfynydd nuclear power station, which began to supply power to the grid system in 1965 and which takes 159 million litres every hour from the lake as a circulating coolant.

Emerging from the north-western side of Trawsfynydd lake, the Prysor eventually flows through a rocky ravine and half a mile from the lake falls obliquely, down a hard rock face in the form of Rhaeadr Ddu into a grotto shrouded with broad-leaved trees.

The most convenient approach to Rhaeadr Ddu is to take the A487 out of Maentwrog, turning right after two miles to the signposted village of Gellilydan, turning left a mile after the village and then right down the lane marked '*I'r Rhaeadr*' ('to the Waterfall'). You can park the car near the farm of Ty'n-y-Coed. A stile leads into a canopied woodland path roofed over with oak trees and with the river shouting below. This sylvan approach is one of the dividends of a visit to Rhaeadr Ddu, for the state of the waterfall is now closely geared to how much of the water is being piped from the Trawsfynydd lake to power the electric turbines at the Ffestiniog Power Station. But however much or little water is falling down the rock, the site is singularly attractive and well worth a visit for its own sake. The dark plunge pool of the falls is lit with ochreous tints of red and brown. There is a small sister falls further down known as the 'Raven Falls' (continuing the sombre nomenclature).

The Prysor eventually flows into the Dwyryd, which reaches the sea through crag-crowned hills where the autumn colours of bracken and heather repeat the ochreous and golden tints of the pool of Rhaeadr Ddu.

The River Prysor forms Rhaeadr Ddu half a mile after issuing from Lake Trawsfynydd. It is a depleted waterfall in a beautiful setting.

Rhaeadr Cynfal (93)

(The Cynfal Waterfall)

The village of Ffestiniog is sited in the old county of Merioneth three miles from the slate-quarrying town of Blaenau Ffestiniog and at the head of the Ffestiniog Vale. This is one of the beauty spots of Wales widely visited as part of the Celtic Grand Tour especially in the late eighteenth and early nineteenth centuries. Its rivers fall through rocky gorges, form pools of ochre and gold in secret grottoes and meander through lush meadows, girdled by mountains. Ffestiniog is set high above the lower valley of the Cynfal river, which has carved out a precipitous gorge on the southern side of the village. When Rhaeadr Cynfal is in full cry, one can hear, standing in the old-fashioned square, a very faint sound of falling water.

The approach to the waterfall offers a choice of route. From the square you can pass through a farmyard at the point where the houses end, keeping subsequently to the footstep-marked track and passing through a series of iron wickets until you reach the final approach to the river. Or you can walk to the top of the village along the Dolgellau road and turn right into a lane by the chapel. Both routes join in a common path which skirts the sidelands above the river.

The sound of Rhaeadr Cynfal confirms your arrival as it falls down its three steep declivities of rock. It is not a high waterfall but unique in that its top section falls in an almost perfect arch, like the circumference of a wheel, lighting the arboreal gloom with a whirling wheel of foam. The fall is well served with steps and handrails for safe viewing.

There is a small sister falls downstream, and between the two one finds the symmetrical columnar rock known as Huw Llwyd's Pulpit. During the reign of James I a stentorian voice could be heard above the thunder of the waterfalls, for the midstream 'pulpit' was used for the preaching of sermons, the declaiming of poetry and, more particularly, the practice of devil-raising spells. Practitioner of all three was a retired soldier, Huw Llwyd, who lived nearby in the house called Cynfal Fawr. Thomas Love Peacock has left us in his novel, *Headlong Hall,* an entertaining account of how Huw Llwyd used his magic spells to raise the (five-horned) devil with whom he was wont to hold regular converse. When raising the devil, Huw was safe from the Evil One once he was on his midstream rock because the Devil could not walk or swim through water (something to do with cloven hooves perhaps). Huw Llwyd (1568–1630) of Cynfal waterfall fame was also a considerable poet, and his 'Fox's Counsel' is in the 1977 *Oxford Book of Welsh Verse* (in English).

The River Cynfal produces a whirling 'wheel' of foam in the arboreal gloom.

Rhaeadr-y-Cwm (94)

(Waterfall of the Cwm)

Two miles upstream fom Huw Llwyd's devil-raising sanctuary is Rhaeadr-y-Cwm, where the Cynfal, here hardly more than in its infancy, shows its paces in a waterfall of a different kind. Indeed, it would be hard to conceive of a falls more different from the symmetrically whirling Rhaeadr Cynfal hidden in the tree-canopied gloom of the Cynfal woods, than Rhaeadr-y-Cwm where the river drops over 400 feet in the form of six cascades into the valley below. After its descent of the ravine, the Cynfal valley opens out, with partly afforested sides, areas of heather moorland and a number of riparian meadows through which the Cynfal sometimes meanders peacefully and sometimes rushes along on its journey towards Ffestiniog.

To those who like their viewing made easy, the spectacle of Rhaeadr-y-Cwm can be conveniently enjoyed from a specially built recess near a car-park at an altitude of a thousand feet, near Pont yr Afon Gam, three miles from Ffestiniog along the Ffestiniog/Bala road. For the walker there is an alternative approach to Rhaeadr-y-Cwm along the Cynfal river from Bont Newydd. This leads to Cwm Cynfal farm where you can then strike up the hillside opposite the cataract and descend some distance down the slopes to obtain a closer look at the multiple falls. It should be emphasized that descent beyond a certain point can be dangerous.

Due to the aspect of its long, precipitous descent, Rhaeadr-y-Cwm is a 'two-faced' fall, and throughout most of the day, except for a short period, one side of the ravine remains in deep shadow, presenting the photographer with a tantalizing choice and adding a somewhat forbidding character to the scene. But the precipitous sides of the shadowed ravine are brightened in season with flowering heather with rocky beds of the tall-stemmed, yellow-flowering stonecrop and with glittering patches of large-petalled mountain buttercups.

The River Cynfal which feeds Rhaeadr-y-Cwm rises a few miles away in the lonely moorland lake of Llyn y Dywarchen, where the cry of the curlew is frequently heard in the skies above the desolation of peaty wastes that surround it. It is an area of many mountain tarns, of which Llyn Morynion (Lake of the Maidens), on the opposite side of the road from the cataract, is one of the most striking and certainly one of the most famous lakes of Welsh legend. The name of the lake traditionally commemorates a sort of Celtic equivalent of the rape of the Sabine women, in that it concerns the fabled death of a number of Welsh wives who were carried off by raiders from the cantref of Ardudwy (south of Harlech) but became so enamoured of their captors that, when they were pursued and their captors slain, the women drowned themselves in the lake sooner than return home.

The young River Cynfal tumbles down from the uplands off the Bala/Ffestiniog road.

The Cymerau Falls (95, 96)

The Cymerau waterfalls are sited in a densely wooded glen through which the river has carved its own ravine, where the woodlands which clothe it are among the richest of their kind, with some especially fine sessile oak interspersed with birch and rowan trees. The Coed Cymerau has been a principal site for Welsh woodland research for over a decade.

To reach the Cymerau falls, take the A496 leading from the village of Maentwrog towards Blaenau Ffestiniog. Near the tiny hamlet of Pengwern, where there is a large park/layby, take a footpath leading at right angles off the layby until you reach a small derelict building, after which there is a footpath to the river, where there is an announcement that 'Coed Cymerau' is an official Nature Reserve. Coed Cymerau is in fact a highly sensitive area, where one needs a special permit from the Nature Conservancy to stray from the footpath. On no account must any of the ground-cover plants be disturbed. This Nature Reserve is leased from the Forestry Commission and is a vestigial gem of the deciduous woodlands which once dominated the Ffestiniog Vale. For the ecologists, the Goedol is a uniquely co-operative river, for in the middle of the Reserve it turns through a right angle so that the woodlands can be studied by the research workers from four distinct aspects, south-east, south-west, north-east and north-west.

There are two waterfalls in the Cymerau Nature Reserve, both occurring on the Goedol, which is fed by a rainfall of eighty inches a year. This high rainfall, coupled with the spray of the waterfalls and the dense, dripping oak canopy, particularly on the lower slopes of the sheer ravine, makes it one of the richest waterfall sites in the principality for mosses, liverworts and the growth of epiphytes on the trunks and branches of the trees.

The Cymerau waterfalls are not high, single waterfalls but consist of multiple miniature falls and cascades which are particularly attractive when the river is full, when the upper falls almost engulf an old rustic bridge which allows access to a cottage nearby. It was below the second waterfall that I encountered an angler who told me that the trout in the Goedol, though they were small as is typical of all fast streams, were among the cleanest and brightest-coloured and best-flavoured in the district. He further assured me that trout always take on the prevailing colour of the water environment where they live. Where it flows over a clean, strong bed, as in the Goedol, they will be bright in colour as well as wonderful to eat. He showed me a pool with overhanging leafy trees, with a high population of various ferns and a bank of heavily lichened boulders, and swore that the trout in that pool had taken on some of the dark green colour which dominanted their environment.

A small waterfall in the luxuriant surroundings of the Nature Reserve of Coed Cymerau. There are two Cymerau waterfalls.

LLE
CYFYNGEDIG
LIMITED
CLEARANCE

The Tanygrisiau Waterfalls (99)

Despite the inevitable landscape desecration—one ton of finished slate for roofing left fifteen tons of slaty debris to litter the landscape—Tanygrisiau, a former slate-mining village in the old county of Merioneth, still retains a certain countryside charm. This is especially true when, after heavy rain, the surrounding heights are lit with ephemeral cataracts descending like roaring white snakes into the valley. Heavy rain also brings into full cry the main Tanygrisiau Waterfall, which is a famous local feature of the upper part of the village.

To reach the Tanygrisiau waterfall, walk up the village street until you see a shakily painted white notice directing you along a lane to the Ffestiniog Railway Station. It could with equal relevance carry the familiar Welsh notice '*I'r Rhaeadr*' ('To the Waterfall') for the Tanygrisiau waterfall descends and lands just a few yards from the Tanygrisiau Station on the narrow gauge line.

The station waterfall is formed by a mountain stream which issues from Llyn Cwmorthin on the northern slopes of the Moelwyn Mountain range. (Llyn Cwmorthin and its setting were hailed by the eighteenth century Thomas Pennant in his *Tour in Wales* as one of the loveliest cwms he had encountered.) After leaving the lake, the stream shows its paces in a spumy series of slides and cascades to fall thirty feet into the plunge pool and when in spate to slap with flecks of foam the windows of the Ffestiniog Railway coaches—pulled by *Prince, Princess, Merddan Emrys, the Earl of Merioneth, Blanche* or *Linda*—just before they pull up at the posh new Tanygrisiau Station. The stream then passes under the tiny railway bridge on its way to the lower reservoir of the Tanygrisiau CEGB pumped storage scheme. The mountain environs of the station waterfall contain other cascades and small waterfalls, and there is one which also falls almost onto the narrow-gauge line a few hundred yards from the main waterfall. None of the little Welsh railways, not even that of Talyllyn where it crosses the viaduct of the Dolgoch glen or stops to take on water at the Dolgoch Falls Station (page 127), regales its passengers with such close displays of white water.

Tanygrisiau today is a unique blend of old and new, an admixture of industrial archaeology and modern high technology. The village lives in the shadow of Blaenau Ffestiniog where the mountain has been disembowelled for its slaty treasure. The discarded entrails piled on gigantic heaps of debris from a century of slate mining and quarrying, where guided tours of the excavated mountain are now a visitor lure, are enlivened by demonstrations of the old slate-finishing skills by veteran craftsmen. Above Tanygrisiau itself the walls of Moelwyn Mawr soar and loom like a gigantic cathedral showing the mining scars and hollows, the bridle ways, the steps and

The Ffestiniog Narrow Gauge Railway is unique in that it has a waterfall virtually in one of its stations.

stairways of stone—the name Tanygrisiau means 'beneath the stairs'—while the environs of Llyn Cwmorthin are scarred and marred with the dereliction and ruin which the slate-extraction epics of Wales have left on the landscape.

The Tanygrisiau pumped water scheme which exploits the power of falling water also has an epic quality. But there the comparison ends, for the CEGB have achieved their industrial purposes with laudable concern for landscape amenity as a genuine priority. The scheme for generating electricity, which exploits the power of falling water which gives the natural waterfall such unique appeal, is based on the use of two reservoirs established at different levels. The upper reservoir is sited high on the flanks of the Moelwyn mountains where Llyn Stwlan, a typical corrie lake, has been enlarged and dammed with a barrier 800 feet long, about a mile above the lower reservoir. This lake receives an annual average rainfall of over 100 inches. The lower reservoir has been formed by the construction of a curved dam across the outlet basin of the River Ystradau near Tanygrisiau, where the dam has been very effectively camouflaged by using the excavated spoil along the downstream face.

A press of the button begins the passage of this great man-made waterfall from Llyn Stwlan through gigantic pipes to the turbines of the power station which has been built in local stone on the west side of the Ystradau reservoir. The water falls into the turbines at periods of peak daytime electricity demand and then collects in the lower reservoir. At night, when the electricity demand is low, the flow is reversed and the same water is pumped back into the upper reservoir.

Unlike some other hydro-electric schemes in Wales in which waterfalls have been immolated, the station waterfall of Tanygrisiau is safeguarded for posterity, for the flow of water in streams above the station is metered, and the amount of compensation water is automatically adjusted so that the flow of water in streams below the (power) station is the same as if the pumped storage system had not been constructed.

A delightful dividend of the giant generating scheme which involved the creation of the new lower lake in the twin reservoir scheme was the renewal of a lease of life to the old Ffestinog Slate Railway, now once again alive and merrily whistling, as it passes through glorious countryside. For when the new reservoir drowned the remains of the old narrow-gauge railway, a new line and a 300-yard-long tunnel were created, roughly parallel to, but above, the previous route, to bring the little train past the waterfall to its stopping-point at the new Tanygrisiau Station.

The Tanygrisiau Waterfall formed by a mountain stream issuing from Llyn Cwmorthin on the northern slopes of the Moelwyn range.

The Conwy Waterfalls (97, 98, 108)

To reach the main Conwy falls, the easiest approach is from the Conway Falls Hotel (designed by Clough Willliam Ellis) which is sited by the turning to Penmachno off the Bettws-y-Coed/Pentrefoelas road. There is a small turnstile charge, but as the autumn advances into winter the visitors disappear and one can approach the falls in peace.

The steep descent to the famous scene is flanked by some fine old woodlands which clothe the surrounding screes and extend along the bank of the river,, to remind one that Nant Conwy was once famous for its oak trees. As early as the reign of Queen Elizabeth I the waters of the Conwy were used to float big oak logs down to the coast, and records of the Gwydyr estates in Nant Conwy report that £50,000 worth of oak was carried by the waters of the river in the six years from 1754. Even today some of the fine native oaks are to be found above the 'Fairy Glen' through which the river charges after the chasm of the Conwy falls.

There are good viewing-places from which to enjoy the spectacle. Having poured down the narrow top part of the gorge, cutting deeply through the fissile argillacious (hard clay) rock, the river is divided at the base by a small rocky islet, so that the two outstretched arms of the pounding river have torn out wide side recesses which the separating torrent fills with foam before the river becomes again a wide, unified frenzy of white water tumbling down the 'Fairy Glen'. This is a grossly 'touristy' misnomer for the magnificently wooded lower Conwy defile.

Though this is its most dramatic waterfall, a mighty torrent of white water surpassed by few Welsh rivers when it is in spate, the Conwy produces other, gentler falls in its upper reaches. The river which enters the sea at the Gwynedd town of Conwy, after an eventful life of twenty miles, has its source in Llyn Conwy, 1,488 feet above sea-level. The lake is three miles to the north of Carnedd Iago, which dominates the surrounding boggy areas, the source of many small streams, most of which eventually find their way into the Conwy river. The lake was for centuries famous for its trout, jealously preserved by the Lords of Penrhyn, the slate-quarrying Kings of Snowdonia. It is now the property of the National Trust, who also have the fishing rights and own the main waterfall gorge and the Fairy Glen.

The National Trust environs of the infant Conwy, the Migneint (the Place of Swamps), is one of the largest moorland wildernesses in Wales, rich in flowers and plants, in birds and ecological interest, in the distant shadow of the two Arenigs. In early spring it is one of the finest gathering-grounds in Wales for flocks of curlews, whose shrill calling acquires new vibrancy in the spring. The curlew finds the Migneint with its stretches of moor grass, deer's hair sedge, the concealing rushes along the

Amid the solitary expanses of the Migneint moor, the infant River Conwy produces a number of small waterfalls.

streams that flow through the hummocks of disintegrating peat, the heather and sphagnum moss and especially the wealth of cotton grass, the ideal place to set up its nest. For the waterfall bounty-hunter walking in the Migneint there can be no greater felicity than to find a waterfall and a nesting curlew in the same line of sight in the spring. The deep pectoral mounds of sphagnum moss, vivid green, white and brown, make a walk over the drier areas of the Migneint a positively sensuous experience.

Brought into early riverhood by many tributary streamlets, the Conwy makes several little waterfalls below Pont ar Gonwy, where the road from Ffestiniog to Ysbyty Ifan crosses the young stream. These waterfalls occur in particularly floral settings where the soil on the more sheltered rocky ledges is luxuriantly colonized with honeysuckle and heather, bilberry, crowberry and numerous ferns, even sometimes with summer bluebells. After its early waterfalls the Conwy still continues to flow through a narrow glen cut out of the rocks, but at Blaen-y-Coed it is joined by the River Serw from near Arenig Fach, and the Conwy flows towards the village of Ysbyty Ifan, where its course becomes more leisurely through agricultural land, with some fine birch groves.

Ysbyty Ifan takes its name from a hospice founded in the early twelfth century by the Knights of St John to provide safe lodgings and succour for travellers benighted on the inhospitable moorland tracks on the upper Conwy, and the hospice was granted various privileges, immunities and the right of sanctuary by the rulers of Gwynedd; these disappeared with the dissolution of the monasteries, but the right of sanctuary and immunity attaching to the land remained, so that the area became a 'safe' place for brigands—a section of the fifteenth-century building where the malefactors gathered is still standing.

When the Conwy, charged with water from its tributaries, especially the Machno, makes its thunderous descent down the precipitous chasm of the main falls, it presents an impassable obstacle to the upward migration of salmon and sewin. The remains of an old salmon ladder placed in position a long time ago were visible until quite recently but have now virtually disappeared. The building of a new salmon pass up the Conwy falls has been investigated by the National Trust, but formidable problems of multiple rights have to be solved before the work can begin.

Fed by the Machno and other rivers, the Conwy rushes down the Conwy gorge where a new 'salmon pass' is being built. It is National Trust property.

The Waterfalls of Pont Cyfyng (112)

(Bridge of the Gorge)

Pont Cyfyng, between Capel Curig and Bettws-y-Coed, does not qualify for inclusion in the main Bettws-y-Coed league of bridges, as do Pont-y-Pair, Pont ar Lledr, which carries the old road to Penmachno, and the famous Waterloo bridge across the Conwy. Probably built as a carriage road about 1800, it is a single-arch bridge with a thirty-four-foot span carrying a road twelve feet six inches wide, with two-foot parapets. But for many Pont Cyfyng is a more familiar name than any of its more illustrious fraternity.

In the first place, it has the finest waterfall show of any bridge in Gwynedd. At Pont Cyfyng the Llugwy, powered by its gradient from the mountains, swollen by feeder tributaries, is hemmed in by constricting walls of hard black rock which have defied its erosive might, confining it into a narrow bed, laced with fangs of rock. The principal fall occurs near the bridge but the river continues to leap and crash on the rocks and boulders for thirty yards or more. The stone wall which leads to the bridge from the Bettws end has recesses—originally included for pedestrian refuse when carriages filled the narrow road—which afford convenient spots for enjoying the spectacle of the waterfalls.

The waterfalls and rapids serve another, more dynamic function than mere spectacle for they form one of the best and most easily accessible stretches of water in the principality for wild water canoeing. Canoeing has been one of Britain's fastest-growing water sports, and the most exciting part of the canoeist's skill and daring is the conquest of wild waters like those at Pont Cyfyng. Pont Cyfyng also has the advantage of offering the canoers a 'graded' challenge, for wild (white) water is graded from 1 to 6 in ascending order of difficulty. Grade 6, which is assigned to the Llugwy waterfalls immediately after the bridge, is chillingly described by aficionados as negotiable only, 'with danger to life and limb'. But the commonly used Pont Cyfyng stretch is graded at 2–3, and the lower part has a Grade 1 rating, ideal for beginners.

Pont Cyfyng is also famous as the turning-point off the Bettws-y-Coed/Capel Curig road for the ascent of Moel Siabod (2,860 feet). A favoured route takes one along the road past the upper slate quarries, the old quarry pools and abandoned buildings to the wild lake on the cwm edge with its morainic debris and piles of boulders. The final climb is along the rocky edge of the cwm. The view from the summit is breath-taking.

The waterfalls on the River Llugwy at Pont Cyfyng near Capel Curig, a favourite spot for 'wild-water' canoeing.

Rhaeadr y Wennol (113)

(The Swallow Falls)

Despite the turnstiles, the spectacle of the Swallow Falls remains undiminished. It is sited about three miles along the road from Bettws-y-Coed to Capel Curig and is one of a number of waterfalls—though incomparably the finest—produced by the River Llugwy in its tempestuous course from Snowdonia to the Conwy.

The Llugwy rises in Cwm Llugwy near the curiously named precipices of Ysgolion Duon (the Black Ladders) in the shadow of Carnedd Llewelyn. A half mile from its source it enters Ffynon Llugwy, now a captive reservoir. At Pont Cyfyng near Capel Curig it produces the first of a series of waterfalls, a foretaste, as it were, of the masterpiece three miles away.

The Swallow Falls are unusual in the sheer extent of their fortissimo performance, which extends for almost half a mile of the boulder- and crag-strewn bed. The approach of the river to the final gorge is highly dramatic, and it is wide because the erosive river has here eaten into the shale sides of the ravine, after which the rush of water is forced into a narrow, high-sided chasm of hard rock into which it falls in a maelstrom of spume and spray.

Tumbling water on this scale has to be seen and heard to provide anything like a true measure of its power. It would certainly need a Turner to capture its truth and, though many have tried, no painter of consequence seems to have succeeded in the task. It has also inspired a number of writers to make the attempt in words. Theodore Watts-Dunton, a friend of Rossetti and William Morris, the protective 'guardian' of Swinburne and a life-long lover of Snowdonia—which he celebrated in his novel *Aylwin*—described the falls in true romantic style:

> *Following the slippery path as far as it led down the dell I stopped at the brink of a pool about a dozen yards, apparently, from the bottom and looked up at the water. Bursting like a vast belt of molten silver out of an eerie wilderness of rocks and trees, the stream as it tumbled down the high walls of cliff to the platform of projecting rocks around the pool at the edge of which I stood, divided into three torrents which themselves were again divided and scattered by projecting boulders into cascades before they fell into the gulf behind. The whole seemed one wide cataract of living moonlight . . .*

George Borrow too, who was a close friend of Watts Dunton, visited the Swallow Falls during his journey through *Wild Wales*. After a lyrical description of the waterfall, he concludes: 'Such is the Rhaiadr y Wennol or Swallow Fall: called so from the rapidity with which the waters rush and skip along.' Borrow was wrong about this for, although it is now universally adopted, it appears the modern name of Rhaiadr y Wennol (Falls of the Swallow) is in fact a corruption of the original Rhaiadr Ewynol which means 'the Foaming Falls'.

The River Llugwy (River of Light) approaches the gorge along a long jagged-rock stretch of river.

Borrow and Watts Dunton were of course able to enjoy the scene when the waterfall was set in solitary woodland surroundings. It must have been a splendid sight, roaring and pouring through its gorge, amid the surrounding woodlands of sessile oak and ash, rowan and sycamore, birch and beech. An area not far from the Swallow still contains a small beechwood which in spring and autumn affords a reminder of the deciduous beauty of the wooded valley before the trees were felled and the areas replanted with conifers.

For the visitor who wishes to approach the falls through the back way, as it were, without the commercial impediment, there is a trail laid out by the Forestry Commission which leads from the entrance to the forest road, about 200 yards from the Towers outdoor pursuit centre, on the minor road from Ty Hyll (the Ugly House) to Gwydyr. This is essentially a forest walk designed to incorporate numerous tree species but eventually passes through the Llugwy Gorge with some fine views of the falls.

Many Welsh waterfalls have legends attached, but that of the Swallow is signally grisly. It states that the spirit of Sir John Wynn (1553–1627), a member of the great Wynn family which occupied Gwydyr Castle, is imprisoned under the falls. It is not surprising that the expiation by waterfall should take a long time for Sir John had a formidably large aggregate of misdoings to exorcise. He was a notorious practititioner of nepotism and a constant conspirer and litigant against both his neighbours and his tenants, in the course of which he was able to build the great estate of Gwydir where Queen Elizabeth is thought to have stayed. His waterfall purgatory has already lasted nearly four centuries but his spirit is doomed to remain imprisoned under Rhaiadr y Wennol until his guilt has been expiated in full and his spirit finally cleansed by the waters.

The descent of the Llugwy through the gorge above Bettws-y-Coed is an avalanche of white water.

Rhaeadr Garth (111)

(The Garth Waterfall)

The upland hamlet of Rhiwddolion, sited a mile and a half south-west of Bettws-y-Coed, gives its name to a little river, the Rhiwddolion, which flows through hilly country for about two miles before passing under the A5 to join the Llugwy. Opposite the entrance to the Miner's Bridge, the stream enters a small Forestry Commission glen in a collection of miniature waterfalls, falling down a forty-foot hard rock protuberance. The waterfall is known locally as Rhaeadr Garth. This is a waterfall glen with a difference for it has been laid out by the Forestry Commission for the convenience and enjoyment of handicapped visitors, for those of limited mobility, the visually handicapped and those who are totally blind.

The Garth Falls was chosen because the paths alongside the river to the waterfall are relatively level, whereas other possible 'trails' investigated in the Gwydyr Forest would have necessitated steep alignments, unsuitable for the elderly and handicapped. The Garth waterfall glen is easily accessible from the A5, with its own small car-park attached about a hundred yards from the road.

The waterfall approach has been planted to incorporate the qualities of a high forest walk. The trees, principally Norway spruce planted in the 1920's, are widely spaced as the result of previous thinning and have been allowed to grow on well beyond the normal forest rotation. As a consequence many of the boles of the trees can be touched by those with impaired or absent vision as they walk down the glen. The wide spacing has also allowed sunlight to penetrate to ground-level, and this has encouraged the growth of a small layer of hazel, holly and rowan. The layout also encourages the presence and nesting of birds.

The three hundred yards to the waterfall have been paved for the easy passage of invalid chairs, either self-propelled or pushed, and for the use of walking-aids. The paved walk is enclosed on either side with handrails and also incorporates a slight meander to break monotony. There are a number of seats and passing-points, and inscribed Braille plates are let into the guide rails to provide information about the forest environment for readers of Braille.

It is deeply enjoyed by blind visitors. Half a century ago a French professor of literature, blind from childhood, wrote these words about the forest, which have significance for the sympathetic Garth design: ' . . . the forest is so cool, one feels the . . . air in the evening and the faintly wafting aromas. There are the resinous odours which vivify the brain, the springs which surprise, the mossy waterfalls which make their coolness felt and which soothe the mind and senses. Although nothing can truly compensate the blind for the sunsets and vast horizons, the forest lifts the soul, as it were, above itself. . . .'

The River Rhiwddolion enters the Garth glen as Rhaeadr Garth, near Bettws-y-Coed. The glen has been laid out by the Forestry Commission for use by the handicapped.

The Waterfalls of Pont-y-Pair (110)

(Bridge of the Cauldron)

The majority of Welsh waterfalls are found in the countryside, and mostly in solitude, but in a few instances they take to the town, even muting the blare of the High Street with their thunder, refreshing the passers-by with time to stand and stare.

It is appropriate that the little town of Bettws-y-Coed, with a hinterland remarkable for its crags and forested heights and for the drama and the diversity of its falls, should have a waterfall near the main street. As at Pont Cyfyng, it is formed by the River Llugwy, which roars through Bettws-y-Coed like a stampede of white mustangs.

Rivers often put on their best white-water displays where the river bed narrows, which is also the logical cost-cutting site for the river to be bridged, and this is so at Bettws-y-Coed, where the Llugwy is crossed by the historic Pont-y-Pair, carrying the old road to Llanwrst and Conwy, with its arches supported on solid rock. Here, in its racing passage through the town, the river is confronted with intrusions of hard rock and big boulder obstacles which produce a fine spectacle of broken water. Pont-y-Pair itself adds to the spectacle of its passage for it is a historic bridge built around 1468 by a local craftsman named 'Howell Saer', described as a 'mason from Penllyn' (though the use of the word 'saer' today is used almost exclusively to signify 'carpenter'). The early bridge has been widened by nine feet on the upstream side to carry the present road, which is sixteen feet wide, and it is thought that the great architect Inigo Jones may have been concerned in the design of the modification. For bridge-enthusiasts Pont-y-Pair is described in the Caernarfonshire section of the *Royal Commission Ancient Monument Report* of 1960 as ' . . . of five arches, the middle one of which spans the deep stream . . . all built of roughly square slabs laid in mortar and in each case [with] the extremities . . . outlined by a regenerating course of thin slabs projecting slightly, from which the wall of . . . rubble rises vertically . . . '.

Of particular interest in the above description is the reference to the 'deep stream' which is spanned by the central arch, For the combination of deep water and rocks which produce the waterfalls has also made the bridge a fine vantage-point from which to watch leaping salmon and sewin in their journey upstream to spawn. From hours of watching at Pont-y-Pair it would seem possible that jumping fish may sometimes make a sort of reconnaissance leap before the final attempt. At Pont-y-Pair salmon-trout have been observed leaping vertically into the air as though to reconnoitre the nature of the obstacle, after which the next attempt has taken them in an oblique trajectory over the falls.

The waterfall at Pont-y-Pair where the Llugwy thunders through the little town of Bettws-y-Coed.

The Waterfalls of Cwm Y Llan (102)

Cwm y Llan is one of the best-known Snowdonia cwms. It contains one of the most famous paths to the summit of Snowdon, some fine glacially formed scenery, with particularly dramatic examples of huge 'glacial erratics', and one of the finest white waterfall displays in Snowdonia. On 14 September 1892 these Cwm y Llan waterfalls accounted—indirectly—for the presence of William Ewart Gladstone, then in his eighty-third year (and Prime Minister for the fourth time), delivering a rousing speech to a huge concourse of Welshmen on 'Justice to Wales', a thousand feet up the cwm.

Gladstone had come to Cwm y Llan at the behest of a lifelong friend and fellow Liberal MP, Sir Edward Watkin, Bart, railway tycoon. Watkin had been so enchanted by the Cwm y Llan white-water display that he had built himself a holiday pleasance in the woods at a point where the Cwm y Llan stream falls into the Gwynant valley, 900 feet below. Always avid for fame but also moved by the genuinely altruistic motives which characterized his whole public life, Watkin had brought in his railway navvies to build a path to facilitate the ascent to the summit of Snowdon. Gladstone had agreed to dedicate the new 'Watkin Path' which ran from where the old cart road (used for hauling quarried slates) ended, to the western side of the Lliwedd ridge and on and up through Bwlch y Saethau to join the Beddgelert path to the Abode of Eagles.

On the afternoon before the ceremony, Gladstone and his wife turned into the entrance leading to Cwm y Llan at Pont Bethania to spend the evening guarded by the village bobby in the Watkin 'Chalet', entertained by the Porthmadoc male voice choir, mingling its harmonies with the waterfalls after heavy rain. The following morning the VIPs drove in a landau to a magnificent glacial boulder, carpeted and roofed in the heart of the cwm, for the official opening. The *Caernarfonshire Herald* for that week describes the scene:

> *After lunch, people began to clamber up the steep path to Sir Edward's mountain home or 'Haffotty' in the vernacular, and passing the cosy little corrugated house on the right, rounded the spur of a lower hill to a scene of the greatest grandeur. On every side, mountains raised their weather-beaten heads, while down their sides foamed innumerable waterfalls. Up a path of muscle-trying steepness, the 'new road' wends its way, passing a significant fan-shaped fall, the last of a chain of cascades, and then the vast open ampitheatre of Cwm y Llan burst into view. In the centre of this vast auditorium rose a huge glacial boulder and, on this, a substantially constructed stone platform, boarded over and carpeted, had been erected. Round this point by about four o'clock gathered some 2000 or 2,500 people, hundreds of whom had come by obscure mountain paths, to see and hear Mr Gladstone . . .*

Gladstone's visit to Snowdonia in his 83rd year was indirectly connected with the white water of Cwm y Llan, now part of the Snowdon National Nature Reserve.

The afternoon was spent in singing Welsh hymns and in political speeches and it was late evening before the concourse streamed down the Gwynant valley.

The octogenarian PM spent a second night at the Watkin chalet and the following morning set out to conquer Snowdon in a horse-drawn landau. The *Caernarfon Herald* again describes the scene:

> *About 11 o' clock a party set out from the Chalet with the intention of ascending to the top . . . Edward Owen the experienced and chief guide of the Goat Hotel, Beddgelert was chosen as guide and co-ordinator. . . . The ascent to the carriage road was leisurely made by Polly, the mettlesome cob of Sir Edward Watkin, drawing up the laudau in which the ladies of the party took turns in riding. When the Path commenced, Tommy a sure-footed pony from the stables of the Goat Hotel was called into requisition, Mr Gladstone riding for a considerable distance. Tommy it should be stated was the first pony that ever ascended Snowdon by this path. When Bwlch y Saethau was reached . . . a heavy cloud of mist . . . swept over the top and enshrouded it for a considerable time. Mr Gladstone did not fear the steepness of the path, but when he saw the mist, he yielded to the entreaties of the ladies, not without regret, to proceed no further.*

So the PM just failed to add his name (with Tommy's help) to the conquerers of Snowdon.

In the decades since, thousands of visitors have turned right precisely where the PM's carriage left the Bethania Bridge on that September evening, and followed him up the mountain on that same path. Watkin had always sought to bequeath his name to posterity. (He had started excavating the Channel tunnel until, after a mile, his under-water activities were halted by a special Act of Parliament.) One of the foremost architects of the Grand Central railway network, he dreamed of a railway joining his native Manchester direct with Paris, a railway tunnel between Scotland and Ireland, a ship canal between Galway and Dublin. He even began to build a 'Watkin Tower' at Wembley on the pattern of the Eiffel Tower. (This failed and was demolished.) In the end he attained enduring fame through his love of waterfalls, for after the ceremonial opening in the cwm two new permanent features appeared on the Ordnance Map—the Gladstone Rock and the Watkin Path.

The river is still cutting its way through the rock, albeit with infinite slowness, making little hollows below each waterfall step.

The Waterfalls of Cwm Merch (105, 106)

A visit to the Watkin Path waterfalls in Cwm y Llan should also take in the waterfalls of its neighbour, Cwm Merch. These twin, adjacent Snowdonia cwms have much the same sort of relationship to each other as Rhaeadr Fawr and Rhaeadr Fach. Cwm Merch too is the poor relation of a rich and glamorous neighbour, but as with Rhaeadr Fach the ensuing neglect is part of its charm for it has remained pristine, lonely, safe from the damage of human feet.

Cwm Merch is part of the Snowdonia Nature Reserve, and the river which provides its name, the River Merch, is a principal tributary of the Glaslyn. The easiest approach to the cwm is as for Cwm y Llan. From Pont Bethania, which crosses the Glaslyn where one parks, turn right into the steep heavily wooded rhododendron-flanked lane leading to the Watkin Path but instead of continuing towards the Path waterfalls, take the road towards the farm of Hafod-y-Llan, skirting the farmyard and passing over a footbridge at the confluence of the rivers Merch and Cwm y Llan on their way to join the Glaslyn. After heavy rain this is a place dominated by roaring rivers, swollen by white mountain water from the twin cwms, a tumultuous watersmeet.

As you begin the ascent of Cwm Merch past a little chalet in the woods, the noisy progress of the River Merch will draw you to the densely wooded left side of the cwm, where the first falls are visible through the shimmering screen of silver birches. At this point near the enchantingly named Clogwyn y Barcut (The Precipice of the Kite) the river falls down a huge midstream crag in a series of white streams. (It is also possible to arrive at this point by starting up the Watkin Path and then skirting the shoulder of the mountain, to arrive eventually at Cwm Merch.)

After the first waterfall the cwm opens out into a wide, steep climb with rocky outcrops and a groundcover of tussocky nardus grass and brown bent, areas of sphagnum moss in the boggy parts, tormentil, butterwort and sundew, and areas of bracken among the boulders. Unlike Cwm y Llan, Cwm Merch has a tree-line from 1,600 to 1,800 feet, mainly oak with sessile characteristics (stalkless acorns, straighter branches, larger stalked leaves), some mountain ash and a small plantation of Scots pine planted earlier for purposes of shelter. Some chestnut trees also grow on the lower slopes but the main tree area of the cwm is just above the Hafod-y-Llan farm which comprises one of the largest permanent ash woods in Snowdonia. An interesting growth on the rocky ridge to the west of Cwm Merch is the mountain juniper, which, though technically a tree, is found here more in the form of a spreading shrub. There are some beautiful specimens growing near the site of the second Cwm Merch waterfall where the fast-flowing river has cut a deep channel in the rock. This juniper foliage gives off a gin-like smell when it is squeezed, and it is from the fully formed, unripe

Below the dense foliage of spring, which includes some juniper trees, the Merch pours down a big outcrop of hard rock.

berry that the famous oil of juniper is distilled which gives gin its flavour.

There is no path proper up Cwm Merch but the going is relatively easy as you climb towards the source of the river which originates about 1,900 feet up between the peaks of Gallt y Wenalt and the jagged Snowdonia spur of Y Lliwedd, at 3,000 feet. The higher waterfalls of the cwm are in fact visible after heavy rain from the park at Pont Bethania, and in full cry this spectacle of white water on the mountain, seen from the road, invariably brings to my mind 'The White Cascade' poem by W. H. Davies (page 29). As you near the top falls, you have to ford the river to get round a big grassy bluff before arriving at the waterfalls. This display of white water covers a mile of river which falls in a series of glacial steps from the lip of the corrie on the skyline, and after unusually heavy precipitation this is one of the most spectacular river scenes in Snowdonia. The finest fall of the series at the top of the cwm occurs when the Merch falls more or less vertically over an igneous dyke intrusion which has resisted the down-cutting of the steeply descending river. The annual rainfall on Cwm Merch is 160–180 inches per annum.

Round these high-altitude falls, you are most likely to find the grazing ruminants which seek a living on the slopes of Cwm Merch. The edible grasses are shared between the principality's two hardiest classes of livestock, the Welsh Mountain sheep and the herds of feral goats, surviving groups of the great herds of milking goats which once formed part of the transhumance farming of Snowdonia. Wales now has the highest population of sheep of any part of Great Britain, and in Snowdonia only the hardy Welsh Mountain breed can cope with the bitter rigours of climate and terrain. The area near the waterfalls on the lip of Cwm Merch is also recognized spring 'rutting' territory of the feral goats, a group of which has its principal summer pasturage on the high slopes of Lliwedd and its main wintering quarters in the woodland areas around Beddgelert. A hoped-for dividend of a springtime visit to the upper Cwm Merch waterfalls is the spectacle of the great horned leader, the shaggy, dark-coloured king of the forty strong Cwm Merch herd, the monarch of the cwm, standing like an ibex above the white water.

The upper waterfalls of Cwm Merch are in the 'rutting area' of a herd of Snowdonia wild goats. The top falls are visible from Pont Bethania.

Rhaeadr Ogwen (117)

(The Ogwen Waterfall)

About fifteen miles south of the village of Aber, between the village of Capel Curig and the small town of Bethesda, the boulder-strewn Ogwen Falls foam and thunder into Nant Ffrancon, with its glacier-hewn-and-strewn sides of barren rock. Nant Ffrancon constitutes the upper part of the Ogwen Valley, one of the glacier gems of Snowdonia.

Rhaeadr Ogwen is formed by the junction of the Idwal and Ogwen rivers, both of which rise in lakes nearby, the Idwal a mile away under the Glyders, the Ogwen a few yards away in Llyn Ogwen traditionally one of the lakes claimed to be the one into which Sir Bedivere of the Round Table cast Excalibur, King Arthur's legendary Sword of Light.

The river, emerging from Lake Ogwen, flows under the Ogwen Bridge which spans the A5 and within a few yards joins the Idwal river to fall 200 feet down the great glacial step at the head of Nant Ffrancon into the deeply ice-hollowed valley below. Rhaeadr Ogwen is unique among Welsh waterfalls in being surrounded by such a striking congregation of high mountains. Rising from the road on the north is the boulder-strewn peak of Pen yr Ole Wen, a route to the Snowdonian giants of Carnedd Llewelyn (3,485 feet) and Carnedd Dafydd (3,437 feet). On its east there towers the mighty three-pointed peak of Tryfan (3,010 feet).

The Ogwen Waterfall is also historically unique as a former watering- and staging-post for the droving of Welsh Black cattle from Welsh hill farms to the fattening pastures of Kent, Essex and the Midlands, and to the London cattle fairs of St Bartholomew and Barnet. For over three hundred years, up to the end of the eighteenth century, the thunder of the falls mingled with the noise of bellowing beasts and the clank of iron as the smiths shod the thousands of cattle for the long journey to feed the growing urban populations of England. The droves often included herds of the hardy Welsh mountain ponies, traditionally known as 'Merlins', which also found a ready market in England. The easy availability of water was the vital factor in the choice of the drovers' staging-posts, and Rhaeadr Ogwen was an obvious choice of over-night rendezvous.

Llyn Ogwen is one of the big Snowdonia lakes most under imminent sentence, not this time from man but because of the silt and other debris which is brought down into the lake by the little River Bochlwyd from the lake of that name in the hanging valley about 800 feet above. Already Lake Ogwen is reduced in depth to approximately six feet with a maximum of a mere ten feet at its greatest depth.

The sudden glacial trough end below Lake Ogwen down which the rivers Ogwen and Idwal plunge over 200 feet.

The Cwm Idwal Waterfalls (114, 115)

Entering Cwm Idwal from opposite the Ogwen Cottage Mountain School near the southern end of Lake Ogwen, one is greeted at the footbridge by a boulder-strewn tumult of white water, where the Idwal arrives at the entrance to the cwm, after flowing for half a mile from the lake of the same name. This is one of the most famous of Snowdonia's cwms, gouged by glaciers out of the volcanic rocks of the Glyder mountains—the last ice retreated about 10,000 years ago—with its brooding moraine-impounded lake, overshadowed by great cliffs.

The cascading welcome at the entrance is not typical of the atmosphere and ambiance of the 980-acre Cwm Idwal, which is now owned by the National Trust and leased to the Nature Conservancy Council. For the cwm is most often a place of brooding silence, a glacial shrine. On a windless day, with mountains swathed in mist, nothing moves in its seemingly birdless gloom. Only the white skeins of the waterfalls stand out on the great walls of sombre rock above the lake. It is a place of awesome and humbling grandeur.

The Cwm Idwal falls do not rank high as exemplars of the marriage of gravity and falling water. But both, the one threading its way down the Glyder Fawr, west of the Idwal Slabs, and the torrent that falls through the chasm of Twll Dhu (Devil's Kitchen) are the vital agents of Snowdon's most striking floral heritage, much of it unique not merely to Snowdonia but to the whole of Britain.

The waterfall that enters through the north-facing, grim volcanic cleft of Twll Dhu is produced by a small stream overflowing from Llyn y Cwn—at 2,500 feet one of the highest lakes in Snowdonia—which falls and splashes its spray among the ice-hewn jumble of glacial boulders below the chasm. The combination of constant moisture coupled with the cold, northerly aspect and boulders inaccessible to grazing sheep, has produced the famed 'Hanging Gardens' of Cwm Idwal, a collection of rare Alpine plants associated with the last Ice Age. From March onwards, the plant wealth and the luxuriance of these colourful rock gardens in their wet, cold ambiance are moving and awe-inspiring. Seemingly growing literally out of rock, the boulder surfaces are arrayed with pink moss campion, mountain sorrel, purple saxifrage, white-flowered vernal sandwort, alpine meadow rue, Welsh golden rod, pink willow herb and many others. Ferns are found in abundance, and spleenwort, parsely fern and filmy fern seems to grow from every crack and cranny. The progression from bare rock to such floral wealth may take a hundred years to establish, beginning with lichens and followed by mosses. Organic material slowly builds up, seeds begin to germinate on the rock surfaces and ledges and in the crevices. As with Twll Dhu, the rocks of the gully to the right of the volcanic 'Idwal Slabs'—the nursery ground of generations of 'rock

The wall of Glyder Fawr and the chasm of Twll Dhu, containing Snowdonia's finest display of alpine flowers and plants in which waterfalls are key agents.

tigers'—are also rich in Alpines, and this second waterfall gully is home to one supremely rare species, its exact site a secret guarded by the Cwm Idwal warden who protects his 984-acre kingdom with jealous dedication, for a careless boot can destroy a century of plant establishment on the rocks, which is difficult for the inexperienced individual, however well-meaning, to appreciate.

After a period of heavy rain, Twll Dhu and the adjacent waterfall are joined by many ephemeral cataracts plunging to the floor of the cwm from the surrounding mountains and feeding the brooding, pewter-hued tarn of Llyn Idwal. The lake, 1,200 feet above sea-level, about half a mile long, a little over 300 yards wide and with a mean depth of 10 feet (36 feet at its deepest point), has its own dark legend. Named after a son of Owen Gwynedd, a powerful Welsh contemporary of King Stephen of England, Idwal was reputedly drowned in the dark waters by his guardian, Nefyn the Handsome, of Conwy, for which crime Nefyn and all his posterity were degraded to the rank of bondsmen. Following the murder, no bird would fly across its haunted waters, but, the guardian's sin has obviously been expiated, for the lake is now visited by herons and cormorants to fish peaty waters, and whooper swans, pochard and golden eye are seen.

For many years the guardian waterfall of Twll Dhu which renders foot and handholds on its sheer cliffs so crumbly and treacherous, kept the doughtiest of explorers away. A famous early climber of Snowdonia's peaks and traverses wrote of the great cleft: 'This savage chasm imparts an intruding feeling of terror as one stands beneath its great walls, while the thunder of the waterfall and the clouds of spray enhance the aspect of inaccessibility.' Twll Du has been long conquered by the climbers but the waterfall clouds of spray still remain the lifeblood of Cwm Idwal's Hanging Gardens, Snowdonia's unique floral heritage.

Cwm Idwal with Pen yr Ole Wen in the background, photographed from near the waterfall from Llyn y Cwn.

The Waterfall of Ceunant Mawr (116, 118)

(Waterfall of the Great Ravine)

The main Llanberis Waterfall occurs to the south-east of Llanberis in the gorge known as Ceunant Mawr. The approach to Llanberis from Beddgelert takes one down the famous pass, hemmed in on either side by mountainous cliffs, with shattered boulders as large as Welsh country chapels piled in gigantic confusion behind the stone walls that run like petrified serpents down the ravine. The Pass of Llanberis is one of the Snowdonian epics in stone which always fills one with a sense of awe and human insignificance. Even the man-made mountains of slate debris from the Dinorwic quarries, once the biggest in the world, are on a titanic scale, rising a thousand feet above the little town, a giant memorial to the age of scenic vandalism even though the slate residues themselves have been magnificently terraced, almost sculptured, tier above tier by the quarrymen.

The pass is the product of glaciers and faults coupled with the down-cutting action of the Nant Peris river. The Llanberis Waterfall, however, is the creation of another little stream, the River Arddu, which over the aeons has been busy minding its own business, which is the cutting of its own little ravine at the end of a hanging valley and creating its own white landmark among the sombre, tree-clad slopes. The river falls into the valley below in two phases, the first a vertical tumble of forty feet through the trees into a plunge pool, after which it makes a roaring slide of eighty feet at an oblique angle down a channel in the rock face, which, when the river is in flood, becomes a wide spill-over curtain of white water.

To see the falls from the high ground to the south, turn left at the entrance to the town and drive to a parking-place opposite the falls near the Snowdonia Mountain Railway; or to view the waterfall from above, at close quarters, climb more or less parallel to the railway before turning south through the boggy area of a little stream to the head of the falls.

For those who want to enjoy the panorama and the waterfall the easy way, the narrow-gauge railway climbs the 4½ miles to the summit of Snowdon and starts from Llanberis. For the walker, the route to the summit virtually follows the railway, keeping to what was formerly the old 'Pony Route'; you can enjoy the waterfall spectacle for as long as you wish on the way.

Everything about the Llanberis scene is on a gigantic scale. Now a scheme on a scale matching the slate quarries has joined the two lakes, the lower Llyn Peris and the upper Llyn Marchlyn Mawr, in a masterly hydro-electric scheme based on a pumped storage on the pattern of Tanygrisiau in the Vale of Ffestiniog. One casualty of this has been the waterfall on the Marchlyn Mawr. When one looks at man's violation of the one-time glorious Llanberis landscape, one can but say '*Sic transit gloria mundi.*'

The Llanberis Waterfall in Ceunant Mawr has been formed by the River Arddu at the end of a hanging valley.

Rhaeadr Fawr (121)

(The Great Waterfall)

In full cry no Welsh waterfall more dramatically exemplifies the majesty and power of falling water than Rhaeadr Fawr in North Wales. The waterfall occurs in a valley to the south of the village of Aber, by the side of the A5, four miles east of Bangor, looking northwards over the Menai Straits. To reach the waterfall, drive out of the village along a steep, tree-canopied lane which leads to a small parking-place at Bont Newydd two miles away. This is the only entrance to the waterfall valley, now designated the Nature Reserve of Coedydd Aber.

The visitor to Rhaeadr Fawr will find immediate evidence of the welcome awaiting at the waterfall end of the valley. At the bridge where the twin rivers Anafon and Rhaeadr Fawr meet, fast, white water from the Snowdonia Carneddau is a sure indicator of waterfall drama to come.

Rhaeadr Fawr is already visible half-way along the stone-and-grass approach track that leads through the combe but at that point the white curtain hanging from the sky is uncannily motionless and silent. Then, as one approaches, the water starts to move, the sound begins and, when one reaches the falls, the early flecks of flying foam give way to a lancing storm of rain from the maelstrom of white spume thrown up from the deep plunge pool of the waterfall. After a period of torrential rain, up to 50 million gallons of water a day roar with speech-eclipsing thunder down the cliff face of the crag.

Rhaeadr Fawr occurs at this point because of the intrusion of a 'dyke' of hard igneous rock (granophyre, a fine-grained granite with quartz crystals) into the softer shale. Unlike the shale deposits which can be cut into by the river, the granophyre presents an erosion-resistant barrier down which the mountain River Goch has to fall as a waterfall to reach the drainage of the valley below. The setting of Rhaeadr Fawr is majestically appropriate, for the immediate approach to the waterfall is flanked on the left of the track by 300-foot-high screes, littered by fragments of rock dislodged from the cliffs by freezing and thawing, while behind the falls on a fine day one can glimpse the tor-like summits of Bera Mawr 2,600 feet and Bera Bach 2,550 feet. These tors can be reached by negotiating a giddy path well to the left of the waterfall which leads to the sources of the stream and eventually takes one to the Snowdonia peak of Carnedd Llewelyn. But it is a route with hazards and demands care.

Watching Rhaeadr Fawr in full crescendo, it is difficult to conceive of its delightfully different face when in dimuendo mood. When the streams at Bont Newydd are flowing peacefully—and the stumpy-tailed, white-throated dippers can submerge easily to perform their virtuoso walks under the water in their search for food—the surging torrent descent to Rhaeadr Fawr is transformed into gracefully separate skeins of white

A long 'dyke' of hard, igneous rock has been intruded (as molten magma) into the softer rocks. The River Goch has to fall over the erosion-resistant cliff to reach the valley below.

water intertwining on the whorled face of the granophyre. At such times, and especially in spring and early summer, one is often regaled by buzzards hovering above the falls, savouring their aerial dominion, tacking, wheeling, soaring effortlessly with motionless wings on the thermals. Sometimes they are mobbed by groups of ravens which nest on the inaccessible waterfall cliffs, darting in and out as though in rehearsed unison, until the great birds move away in valley-spanning curves.

The waterfall valley has a rich and varied small bird life as well, because its many oak trees are a species uniquely productive in the woodland chain, oak leaves being a favourite food of the winter moth caterpillars and also of the mottled umber moth, both important foods for many bird species, especially the pied flycatchers (for which nestboxes are provided). The Coedydd Aber Reserve also supports green and great spotted woodpeckers, nuthatches, tree creepers, several species of tit, redstarts, wood and willow warblers, while the moors at the head of the valley have ring ouzels, whinchats, wheatears, merlins and kestrels. The woodlands also include the unique sanctuary of 'Wren Goch', an eleven-acre spring-fed alder woodland, one of the few left in Wales, formerly exploited by itinerant Welsh craftsmen who fashioned, on site every spring, thousands of wooden soles for the clog-makers of the region. The Forestry Commission has now afforested some of the approach slopes, mixing the planting of Japanese larch, Norway spruce and western red cedar with broadleaved beech, sycamore and poplar for amenity reasons.

There is evidence of a small settlement on the slopes near the waterfall, consisting of the remains of seven dwellings and two cow byres. Before the Enclosures, dairy cows found good grazing here and were attended by milkmaids from the village who milked the cows and carried the milk two miles back to Aber twice a day.

Rhaeadr Fawr is rewarding to visit at all seasons, but especially when the trees on Maes y gaer, the Iron-Age fort at the valley entrance, and on the valley slopes have donned autumn livery and when the waterfall is roaring a welcome from Creigiau Rhaeadr Fawr at the end of the combe.

The face of Rhaeadr Fawr in drought when the depleted river falls softly down the whorled granite.

Rhaeadr Fach (120)

(The Little Waterfall)

Sited other than as near neighbour to Rhaeadr Fawr, this waterfall would certainly not carry a title implying a waterfall of lesser magnitude, but Rhaeadr Fach lives as it were in the majestic shadow of its Big Brother and pays the penalty.

Perhaps the avenue of access has also contributed to its relative neglect, for to arrive at Rhaeadr Fach one has to wade the river below Rhaeadr Fawr—not at all easy when the river is full—and then climb up the scree to enter the other part of the Aber valley (to be rewarded incidentally with some unusual dramatic views of the top section of Rhaeadr Fawr). From the top of the steep bank above the river, keep to the left side along the track which follows a stone wall and fence, to arrive at the waterfall site after about a mile. Rhaeadr Fach distils an unmistakable atmosphere of loneliness, even desolation. The wildness has not been affected by constant human visitation; the solitude is pristine and undisturbed. This section of valley also forms part of the Coedydd Aber Reserve.

The waterfall occurs when the River Rhaeadr Fach cataracts down its gully to fall in three fine leaps, a descent of about 200 feet, though its profile of fall is not as precipitous as that of Rhaeadr Fawr. The early course of the river, before it takes to the air, is down the northern slope of Bera Bach. Rhaeadr Fach, like its adjacent Big Brother, is produced by the intrusion of a 'dyke' of hard rock into the softer mudstones and shales. Along the junction of the erosion-resistant rock and the shales there is a line of springs which was extensively used by the mountain ponies in the long droughts of 1976 and 1984. There is also an old lead-mine 120 feet long to the west of the falls.

The environs of Rhaeadr Fach contain evidence of early settlement, with vestigial traces of round huts and small animal enclosures, some possibly dating from the late Iron Age and from Romano-British times. The environs of waterfalls are always growthy because of the damp atmosphere from the spray of the falls, and where the Rhaeadr Fach valley flattens out at the top of the falls, there is a tiny cottage shelter, with a fireplace but no window—which was probably used as a '*hafod*', the summer homestead to which the Welsh farmer moved with his livestock onto the higher ground before returning to the main homestead for the winter.

The river which forms Rhaeadr Fach is swallowed up by the Rhaeadr Fawr river a quarter of a mile below the Rhaeadr Fawr Waterfall. The smaller waterfall, lonely and picturesque, adds an additional dimension of pleasure to the delights of Coedydd Aber.

Rhaeadr Fach, a lonely, not much visited waterfall in the shadow of 'Big Brother', but with a distinctive, solitary charm.

PART II

NEATH TRIBUTARY WATERFALL (2)

This is very much a 'roadside waterfall' which tumbles down a steep channel about two miles north-east of Aberdulais on the A465. After its descent the unnamed stream passes under the road and joins the River Neath. The fall is contained in a little wooded dingle which is totally unexpected, at the side of the busy road, near a convenient layby where one can park to walk (carefully) back and climb the few yards to the viewing-point provided. The river descends obliquely, part water-slide, part waterfall.

The waterfall by the side of the A465 before its junction with the River Neath.

 The uppermost waterfall on the Tawe tributary.

TAWE TRIBUTARY WATERFALLS (4 and 5)

These small waterfalls occur on a tributary of the River Tawe which rises on the thousand-foot contour of the Crynant Forest. To reach the falls, take the A474 from Neath toward Pontardawe, turning right at Gelinudd and left at the next crossroads. Continue along this narrow road past the hamlet of Cilybebyll until you reach Crynant Forest (parking). The forest road takes you to the farmstead of Tareni Gleision, where you skirt the farmyard and continue for about half a mile in the direction of the electric pylons until you reach the river and the first waterfall which descends about twenty feet in two stages before charging down the steep-sided valley. To arrive at the second waterfall, the easiest approach is to return to Tareni Gleision and then take the track leading down from the farm to the juction with the Tawe.

CRAWNON WATERFALL (19)

The River Crawnon south of the Talybont reservoir produces a small waterfall in a wooded combe near the abandoned workings of the Cwar-yr-Hendre quarries. To reach the site, turn off towards the village of Llangynidr from the road between Crickhowell and Brecon, passing through the village along Dyffryn Crawnon to the old quarry railway track.

DRINGARTH TRIBUTARIES WATERFALL (21)

To find this waterfall, take the road from Pont Nedd Fechan through Ystradfellte until the first (narrow) road on the right which crosses the River Mellte. Take the road to the first left, which later becomes a private road leading to the Ystradfellte reservoir. The waterfall is formed at the junction of two tributaries of the River Dringarth which after heavy rain actually meet and marry in mid-air. The tiny grotto of this watersmeet is remarkable for the lovely ochreous colours of the stones and gravel in the river bed.

Illustration overleaf

200 *The waterfall at the junction of the Dringarth tributaries which meet in mid-air, when the waters are in full cry.*

LLIA WATERFALL (22)

Any analysis of how the river system of the Vale of Neath developed inevitably refers to the 'ancestral Llia'. It seems that this charming little river was once one of the 'big guns' of the vale until it was captured and cut down to size. The Llia today has a fairly short life from its source on Fforest Fawr at a height of 1,700 feet to its junction with the River Dringarth about three miles away, when both rivers become the Mellte. To reach the waterfall on this colourful little river, where it flows and swirls and dances through grassy sidelands and clumps of flowering gorse, take the minor road which runs from Pont Nedd Fechan to Ystradfellte for three miles, where a picnic site is reached. The Llia runs below the eastern side of the road, and the waterfall is caused by a massive outcrop of sandstone beds along the course of the river, which have resisted erosion. The Llia at this point is one of the most charming little rivers in the Vale.

A waterfall on the Llia caused by some large sandstone outcrops.

BWREFWR WATERFALLS (23 and 24)

These waterfalls occur inside a section of the Talybont Forest. The best approach is from Talybont-on-Usk, from which you take a minor road, signposted Pontsticill. The road skirts the eastern side of the Talybont reservoir and continues along the river for two miles until you find a parking and picnic place on the left side of the road. Cross the road into the 'Forest Trail' and, to reach the first main waterfall on the Nant Bwrefwr, follow the marked steep Forest Trail alongside the River Bwrefwr. This is a narrow waterfall which falls vertically about fifty feet onto a glaciated pavement of rock. The approach to the second Bwrefwr waterfall takes one on a hard, steep climb through the conifers to a small bridge across the river immediately above the second main waterfall falling down a sheer face with numerous jagged points so that the waterfall looks like a white curly fleece.

There's a third small waterfall on the River Bwrefwr further upstream and outside the forest. The river rises at 2,000 feet on Craig y Fan Ddu and makes a lot of white water before its junction with the River Caerfangell on its way to the Talybont reservoir.

Here the mountain stream falls over a jagged precipice in the Talybont Forest.

The main Talybont Forest waterfall falls onto a glaciated pavement of rock.

TAF-FAWR WATERFALL (26)

This waterfall is formed on the River Taf-Fawr which rises on the western side of the Brecon Beacons near the 2,000-foot contour and flows southwards into the Beacons Reservoir. To reach the waterfalls, take the A470 from Brecon towards Merthyr Tydfil, passing the Youth Adventure Centre at the former Storey Arms Inn. The waterfalls are on the left about a quarter of a mile from the Centre where the river comes down the side of the Beacons, with the main waterfall being followed by a series of cascades. This is one of the principal starting-points for the magnificent walk up the Beacons from the southern side.

Falls on the Taf-Fawr river coming off the Brecon Beacons near Storey Arms, the Youth Adventure Centre.

NANT Y BWCH WATERFALL (30)

This waterfall is near Capel-y-ffin (the Boundary Chapel) in the Black Mountains in the old county of Monmouthshire. To reach the waterfall, take the A465 out of Abergavenny to Llanfiangel Crucorney, then the B4423 past Llanthony along the vale of the River Ewyas until reaching Capel-y-ffin. Turn left just before the famous tiny church along a narrow road and farm lane to the farm of Blaen Bwch. You pass farm buildings in your descent to the river and the waterfall, which is hidden in a steep-sided hollow can be heard falling sixty feet down its wide sandstone precipice into the plunge pool. This is one of the few waterfalls on the Black Mountains and can be part of a superb walk to the source of the river, beneath the crags of Rhiw Wen at a height of about 2,000 feet.

Nant y Bwch (the Stream of the Buck) falls into a dark gorge near the village of Capel-y-ffin in the Black Mountains in Gwent

BACH HOWEY WATERFALL (31)

The village of Erwood is sited eight miles south of Builth Wells on the A470 in Powys. There is an attractive waterfall nearby on the River Bach Howey (a tributary of the Wye) which rises 900 feet up at Rhosgoch Common and has cut a deep (heavily wooded) gorge, particularly in the last section of its descent to Erwood. The rock over which the Bach Howey falls about half a mile upstream from its junction with the Wye is called Craig Pwll Ddu, and the waterfall descends obliquely and in two steps over the rocky outcrop in the narrow gorge. The easy approach to the waterfall is to turn off the A470 a mile before the village (coming from Talgarth) across the bridge over the Wye and then to take the left turning along the old railway bridge until the Bach Howey is reached which leads up to the gorge and the waterfall.

CADNEY WATERFALL (32)

The waterfalls on the River Cadney, which joins the River Cnyfiad to become the River Cammarch, are approached from the little town of Beulah along a narrow road leading to Abergwesin. You will find improvised parking just beyond the little wayside church; then take the track which climbs steeply through afforested slops for a quarter of a mile into the valley of the Cadney, as it opens out. Follow the track for half a mile down to the river. The waterfalls are hardly more than rapids and occur on two sections of river.

More a series of rapids than waterfalls (though marked as such on the map) in a solitary, charming section of the River Cadney.

MARCHEINT FAWR WATERFALL (42)

To reach this waterfall on the River Marcheint Fawr, drive from the town of Rhayader toward Llangurig, turning right down the minor road signposted to St Harmon. A mile from the turning, where the river flows under a bridge to join a Wye tributary, strike upstream in a northerly direction. The waterfall is formed about a mile from the bridge falling over a rock face about twenty feet high.

LUGG TRIBUTARY WATERFALL (43)

Perhaps more than any other this is essentially a 'farm waterfall'. The farm lies up a lane just off the B4356 between Llanbister and Crug, along a turning to the left, 1½ miles from Crug. The farmer's guidance is essential, for the falls are difficult to find. About half a mile from the farmstead one reaches a derelict building from which the river can be seen. The waterfall is on a tributary of the Lugg. After descending to the Lugg, cross a ford at a spot where the tributary first comes into sight, and the falls are a few hundred yards further up. Whereas the majority of waterfalls are most attractive when the river is high, these falls, which tumble over a cliff about 25 feet high, are enchanting in drought, when the face of the cliffs is a veritable rock garden of plants. I also remember the walk to this falls particularly well because it went through a field of oats in stook where some marvellous menacing bird-scarers had been artistically made from old coats and broomsticks which in the evening light looked quite terrifyingly real. There was not a rook in sight.

In drought, with just a few streams of water, this waterfall still has considerable charm and a host of 'waterfall plants'.

SEVERN TRIBUTARY WATERFALL (44)

This unnamed waterfall on a tributary of the Severn, to the south of the Hafren Forest, is approached from the little market town of Llanidloes set in the Plynlimon foothills on the A470. After crossing the town bridge over the River Dulas, the road to the falls runs south-west of the town for about a mile, after which you take the left-hand fork, over the River Severn, continuing along the south side of the river for about 2½ miles. After crossing a second bridge, turn left onto a narrow, unfenced steep lane from which after about a mile the waterfall can be glimpsed from the road. It is a hazardous climb down the densely wooded scree to the falls, which are about twenty feet high.

TRAWSNANT WATERFALL (46)

To reach the waterfall on the River Trawsnant, leave the village of Staylittle by the road running west to Felin Dyrnal. From the old mill there is a vestigial track along the western bank of the river, and the waterfall is sited about a mile upstream, where the river is interrupted by a series of hard rocks.

NANT YSGUTHAN WATERFALLS (51)

This is very much a farm waterfall. When I knocked at the front door of the large new farmhouse of Gesail Ddu, the farmer came from round the back of the house carrying a twelve-bore shotgun. There was no minatory intention because he had been walking along the Nant Ysguthan (the Wood Pigeon's Stream) looking for sport. The name also features in Bryn Ysguthan, the Hillside of the Woodpigeon. To reach Gesail Ddu farm one has to negotiate a hairpin bend with a cattle grid off the Llangadfan/Mallwyd road on the A458 about four miles from Llangadfan. To get to the waterfalls from the farmhouse, strike up a sidelane towards a track visible along the top of the escarpment. Then proceed as far as an old stone wall which leads precipitously down to the river where the small waterfalls are just visible. There is another waterfall further upstream.

The Welsh name means 'the Wood Pigeon's Stream'. Reaching the waterfalls involves a difficult scramble.

ALAN TRIBUTARY WATERFALL (52)

To find this waterfall, proceed from the village of Llanfyllin towards Lake Vyrnwy to park at the first telephone kiosk on the right two miles from Llanfyllin, near a small chapel at Tycrwyn. Ask the way at Cwm Euthel farm for the exact point of entrance to a steep, hard track which leads to a derelict farm building. The approach from this point is delightful, particularly in late autumn when one walks over carpets of acorns from the canopy-meeting clumps of Welsh oaks, and over the hundreds of crabapples fallen onto the path. Pistyll y Craig Ddu is just visible from the fence which wards off the near-inaccessible gorge. The true reward is the walk, the return to the road characterized by some breath-taking views.

LAKE VYRNWY WATERFALLS (53 and 54)

Just as the lakes of the Elan valley assuage the giant thirst of Birmingham so the Welsh Lake Vyrnwy supplies Welsh water for Liverpool. It is always possible to cavil at detail but like most of the admirably executed Elan enterprise, the overall effect of Lake Vyrnwy is apposite to the grandeur of the natural scene with perhaps a tinge of Swiss atmosphere emanating from the crag and conifer surrounds. The eastern end of the lake is approached by the B4393 from Llanfyllin, passing through the hamlet of Llanwddyn. To reach the first of the Lake Vyrnwy waterfalls, cross the dam at the east end of the lake, continuing along the road on the south-western side for some two miles. After a left-hand bend in the road the waterfall appears falling obliquely down a hundred-foot cliff before the river passes under the road into the lake. It is a graceful amalgam of waterslide and falls but care is needed by the visitor for there is little space for observation on a very busy road particularly in the holiday season. There is also a number of small cascades on the River Eiddew which flows into the lake at its north-west extremity after a precipitous journey, following its origin 2,000 feet up on the Aran contours.

Illustration overleaf

Above Lake Vyrnwy the Eiddew falls and slides down the hillside before passing under the bridge into the lake.

TRESAITH WATERFALL (65)

An unnamed stream, which rises at 500 feet south of the little spa of Tresaith in Dyfed, falls down a cliff above the beach of Traeth-pen-Bryn.

LOUGHOR WATERFALL (58)

The waterfall on the River Loughor is reached from Llandybie, a small town north of Ammanford on the A483. The waterfall is in the grounds of the Glynhir mansion, which is sited on the left-hand bank of the Loughor river, a mile and a half out from Llandybie. The Loughor, which rises on the westernmost top of the Black Mountain, enters the grounds of Glynhir three miles from its source, falling through a ravine which is densely wooded and overgrown with shrubs, then charging towards Ammanford to enter on a final course of meandering before reaching the sea at the town of Loughor seven miles north-west of Swansea.

SYFYNWY FALLS (60)

The Syfynwy Falls occur at the southern end of the Rosebush reservoir in the Preselly Mountains of Pembrokeshire. The approach is from the New Inn at the crossroads of the B4329 from Cardigan to Haverfordwest. Half a mile south of the New Inn, turn left off the B4329 down a lane which leads directly to the Syfynwy Falls at the southern end of the Rosebush reservoir. The former waterfall has been enveloped by a dam over which, when the reservoir is full, the water falls hundreds of feet with dramatic effect.

MWYRO WATERFALL (66)

To arrive at the falls made by the River Mwyro, make for the carefully preserved ruins of the Cistercian abbey of Strata Florida (the Way of Flowers) about fifteen miles south-east of Aberystwyth, following the B4343 from Ysbyty Ystwyth to the village of Pontrhydfendigaid and on to the abbey. A minor road to the left of the abbey leads to the very remote farm of T'yn-y-Cwm. Here one should park for, though the track to the fall is negotiable, it is terribly rough and stoney. After a walk of about 1½ miles, through a lane loaded each side with hazel trees, the valley opens out into wide, grassy meadows at the end of which the River Mwyro falls over a series of crags. It is difficult to approach the falls (which are relatively insignificant except after heavy rain) because of the extensive fencing to keep the sheep away from the river and from straying.

The little stream falls down a rocky channel in remote, desolate country to the east of the magnificent ruins of the Strata Florida abbey

CARODOC WATERFALL (67)

The Caradoc Waterfall is sometimes credited to Ystradmeurig, the remote hamlet about fifteen miles south-east of Aberystwyth, but it is actually sited in the close-by village of Tynygraig, along the B4340. Here an unnamed village stream, a tributary of the Ystwyth, passes under the village street and within a hundred yards falls over a sheer cliff-face over a hundred feet high into a dark ravine, lighting the gloom with its roaring embroidery. The falling stream is divided into three skeins and can be extremely impressive after rain. The approach to the falls is by an old mill which is now part of a private garden. The falls was referred to by George Cumberland in his 'Attempt to Describe Hafod' (page 115) as '. . . an original cascade, remarkable for its height and surrounding scenery; the place called Cwm Caradoc is saith to have derived its name from a man who rode into it on horseback and was killed, as he well might be by the fall'.

The Caradoc Waterfall falls over a high, sheer cliff face into a dark hollow.

EINION WATERFALL (75)

These falls, sometimes known as the Furnace falls, have acquired a greater popularity than some others which are more dramatic, perhaps because they are literally a few yards from the roadside at the village of the same name. Furnace is close to—almost part of—the village of Eglwys Fach, which is about two miles south of Pont Llyfnant where the River Llyfnant flows under the road from Aberystwyth to Machynlleth, into the estuary of the Dovey. The power of the River Einion and its waterfall was for centuries used to drive the waterwheels for the metal-processing which was concentrated close by. (Hence the village name). The big stone building which still looms over the Einion bridge was the site of the blast furnace—although it is known locally as a barn—used in the manufacture of iron, and the water-power was used to work the bellows. Some of the old furnace equipment still remains, in the ownership of the Department of the Environment. The waterfall was artificially raised to provide a greater head of water, and the waterfall, ensconced in the rock-surrounded pool, has considerable picturesque charm as it tumbles in two streams into the large pool at its base.

FAIRBOURNE WATERFALL (81)

This waterfall is on a tiny nameless stream which rises in the western foothills of Craig Cwm Llwyd at a height of 800 feet. It has a short life of less than two miles, passing through the grounds of Panteimon Hall half a mile from its source, where the small waterfall occurs, two miles south-west of Arthog.

The Furnace falls so called because the head of water was formerly used to drive the bellows to heat the nearby iron-processing furnace.

NANT Y CRAIG-WEN WATERFALLS (83)

This waterfall occurs on a height above the Dolgellau/Dinas Mawddy road (A470) at a point near Pont Buarth Glas where there is a parking lay-by just off the main road. From here a forestry road winds its way along the southern side of the hill until one reaches a bridge over the Nant y Craig-Wen river where there is a magnificent view over the valley of the Dovey and the southern peaks of the Arans. To reach the falling water, climb the river bank above the bridge through dense, wet thickets of hazel and willow until you reach an open space to see the river rushing down and spreading itself over Craig Wen and pouring through a rocky channel under the bridge to its confluence with the River Cerist two miles from its junction with the Dovey.

A visit to this waterfall usually entails a wet shirt from the dense, sodden thickets of hazel and willow.

LLAETHNANT WATERFALL (85)

The name 'Llaethnant' (the Milk Brook) describes the Upper Dyfi during its passage from its source in the Aran lake of Craiglyn Dyfi where it is both an infant stream and marked by milky white rapids and small waterfalls. To reach these early falls, take the Dinas Mawddy road off the Dolgellau/Welshpool road, continuing to the village of Llanymawddy and on to Blaen Pennant Farm. A track by the farm on the left leads from the road along the foot of the steep, rugged slopes on the northern side of the river before the rocky descent, to the river bank close to the series of cascades.

LLIW WATERFALL (90)

To reach this waterfall, take the A494 from Bala to Llanuwchllyn, turning to the right half a mile before entering Llanuwchllyn. It is a very steep and narrow mountain road with few passing-places which goes through the tiny hamlet of Tyn-y-Bwlch, after which it continues to climb steeply for another mile. Park near the farmhouse of Buarthmeini. From here a track leads down to the River Lliw near the shallow gorge where it produces a series of small waterfalls.

CWMNANTCOL WATERFALL (87)

This small waterfall on the Cwmnantcol river, long famous for its trout fishing, is reached from the picturesque village of Llanbedr which is three miles south of Harlech. To reach the waterfall take the narrow road out of Llanbedr, alongside the River Arthog, turning right on to another small road after passing a telephone kiosk. This approach leads along the Cwmnantcol river and the waterfall will be found approximately one mile from the junction of the two rivers.

The simplest form of bridge involves the use of an iron girder such as this, which crosses the River Pyrddin leading to the waterfall of Scŵd Einion Gam.

NANT HIR WATERFALL (91)

Walking along the infant Conwy river over the great wilderness of the Migneint, one is conscious of the Arennig mountains, Arennig Fawr and Arennig Fach, looming on the south-eastern skyline. The Arennig waterfall, Pistyll Gwyn—not to be confused with the similarly named fall of the Arans—occurs on Nant Hir (the Long Stream), which rises at an altitude of over 2,000 feet on the slopes of Arennig Fawr. This is a true mountain stream which after heavy rain flows down the mountainside with the speed of a galloping charger, falling about a thousand feet in just over a mile in its early stages. Nant Hir is one of the many rivers which eventually flow into Lake Bala. To reach the waterfall, leave the A4212 road from Trawsfynydd to Bala at the point where it is met by the B4391 road from Ffestiniog, and proceed along a mountain road toward Llidiardau, turning right a mile after the first telephone kiosk along a track which leads to the eastern side of Llyn Arennig Fawr. After skirting the eastern side of the lake, make the steep, rocky ascent of the Nant Hir Valley until Pistyll Gwyn comes into view, falling over the granite face of Craig Wen (the White Rock) to which the white descent of Pistyll Gwyn has given its name.

HEN WATERFALL (100)

To reach this waterfall on the Hen river, take the A499 from Llanwnda to Pwllheli and after passing through the village of Clynnog-Fawr proceed along a minor road, to park at the farmstead of Cwmgwared. Follow the track through the woods and after a quarter of a mile of steep climbing descend to the river guided by the sound of the small waterfall. The Hen is a small stream rising in a nearby area between the crags of Bwlch Mawr and Gurn Goch and after a short life of only two miles enters Cardigan Bay.

'The Devil's Bridge' which spans the gully of the Mynach is made up of three separate bridges, built at different dates on top of each other, in pick-a-back storeys as it were.

MAESGWM WATERFALL (101)

To reach this waterfall, cross the Dolwyddelan bridge over the River Lledr at its confluence with the Maesgwm tributary. A narrow road follows the course of the Maesgwm and after about a mile a forestry road leads to the farmstead of Tyn-y-Cwm where one can park. The waterfall is a quarter of a mile from this point where the river makes a sharp right-hand bend.

DIWAUNEDD WATERFALLS (103 and 104)

Two waterfalls are marked on the River Diwaunedd, a River Lledr tributary which flows out of Diwaunedd lake and joins the Lledr after two miles. To reach the falls, join the A470 after Bettws-y-Coed to follow the Lledr through the little town of Dolwyddelan, turning right to the old 'Roman Bridge' station and crossing the Lledr before arriving at the village of Blaenau Dolwyddelan. From here continue through the village onto a field track to arrive at a bridge over the Diwaunedd river, where one can park. From the bridge a path leads up the side of the hill towards a farm where you should enquire about the best way up the field sideland to the top of the gorge. The waterfalls can just be seen from the top of the scree, but the precipitous nature of the descent to the river makes it difficult to reach the bank below the falls.

MACHNO FALLS (107)

The falls of the River Machno occur about a hundred yards before its confluence with the Conwy, after a final tempestuous descent down a wild, inaccessible gorge. In recent years the waterfall on the Machno has been upstaged by the spectacle of the Conwy falls though the Machno was once an integral part of the Grand Sightseeing Tour, and in the thirties it rated a charge of a few pence from the cottager whose garden had to be crossed to approach the falls. The garden is still there but there is no gate and no key, and one just asks permission to walk the few paces from the road to see the waterfall. The Machno falls about fifty feet in its first tumble and continues to plummet down the gorge for another hundred feet. There are no safeguards and one should exercise care, for the approach is slippery and uneven. To get to the Machno, turn off the A5 at the signpost marked Penmachno (B4406) and after half a mile turn right by the woollen mill. The cottage by the falls is on the left-hand side after about a quarter of a mile.

The Machno Falls were acclaimed one of the 'Big Three' waterfalls (with the Conwy and Swallow) fifty years ago.

YSTUMIAU WATERFALL (109)

To reach these waterfalls, take the A470 from Bettws-y-Coed to Dolwyddelan, and a hundred yards before the main hotel as you enter the town there is a steep track ascending from the right-hand side, marked towards Capel Curig. After climbing for a quarter of a mile enter on a forestry road which leads to the left to join the river at a point where it produces a series of cascades.

DULYN WATERFALL (119)

This waterfall is on the River Dulyn which joins the Conwy near Tal-y-bont, a small village halfway along the B5106 between Trefriw and Conwy. The waterfall is reached by turning left immediately after the village inn and continuing for half a mile up the road, to park by a left fork. Here engage the left road past some cottages and a uniquely charming village well in the form of a tiny, graceful waterfall. After walking for a few hundred yards take the very steep lane to the right which leads to a magnificent 'tunnel' of hazelnut trees, loaded in autumn, as far as an iron gate, after which follow the river down the precipitous path to the little footbridge across the Dulyn gorge. Here, after a particularly charming walk, the river, which rises at 2,000 feet, charges in numerous cascades over large rock outcrops and boulders and falls progressively more steeply down the wooded gorge. The waterfall can be glimpsed from above but is extremely difficult to reach from below.

226 *The waterfall bird: The Dipper (the water ousel) builds its nests on rocks behind or even beneath the waterfall.*

Part III

List of Welsh Waterfalls and their locations

This list of Welsh waterfalls, given county by county, contains all the waterfalls featured in the 1:50,000 Ordnance maps of Wales and also a number of other waterfalls not marked on these maps but judged worthy of inclusion. (Entries run from South to North).

	Near Place Name	*Name of Waterfall River*	*Waterfall as described on OS Map*	*OS Sheet No.*	*National Grid Ref. No.*	*Page*
	WEST GLAMORGAN					
1	Aberdulais	Dulais	Unmarked	170	SS 772 995	45
2	Ynys-dwfnant	Unnamed	Waterfall	170	SN 804 014	197
3	Resolven	Melin Court	Waterfall	170	826 017	47
4	Crynant Forest	Tributary of Tawe	Waterfalls	160	764 064	199
5	Crynant Forest	Tributary of Tawe	Waterfalls	160	758 066	199
	POWYS					
6	Pont Nedd Fechan	Sychryd	Unmarked	160	918 078	69
7	Pont Nedd Fechan	Sychryd	Unmarked	160	915 080	69
8	Pont Nedd Fechan	Pyrddin	Waterfalls (Scŵd Einion Gam)	160	891 093	51
9	Pont Nedd Fechan	Pyrddin	Waterfalls (Scŵd Gwladys)	160	896 093	49
10	Pont Nedd Fechan	Nedd Fechan	Unmarked (Horseshoe Falls)	160	904 097	59
11	Pont Nedd Fechan	Nedd Fechan	Unmarked (Lower Ddwli)	160	905 098	61
12	Penderyn	Hepste	Unnamed (Lower Cilhepste)	160	927 098	57
13	Penderyn	Hepste	Waterfall (Scŵd yr Eira)	160	928 100	53
14	Pont Nedd Fechan	Nedd Fechan	Unmarked (Upper Ddwli)	160	906 104	61
15	Ystradfellte	Mellte	Waterfall (Scŵd y Pannŵr)	160	923 104	67
16	Ystradfellte	Mellte	Waterfall Scŵd Isaf Clungwyn)	160	924 106	65
17	Ystradfellte	Mellte	Waterfall (Scŵd Clungwyn)	160	925 110	63
18	Coelbren	Nant Llech	Henrhyd Falls	160	854 120	71
19	Talybont Reservoir	Crawnon	Waterfall	161	SO 091 149	199

	Near Place Name	*Name of Waterfall River*	*Waterfall as described on OS Map*	*OS Sheet No.*	*National Grid Ref. No.*	*Page*
POWYS (Continued)						
20	Ystradowen	Twrch	Waterfalls	161	SN 773 154	77
21	Blaentringarth	Tributary of Dringarth	Unmarked	160	946 156	199
22	Castell Goch	Llia	Unmarked	160	928 163	201
23	Talybont Reservoir	Nant Bwrefwr	Waterfalls	160	SO 061 175	202
24	Talybont Reservoir	Nant Bwrefwr	Waterfalls	160	055 177	202
25	Gwyn Arms	Haffes	Unmarked (Scŵd Ddu)	160	SN 830 180	75
26	Storey Arms	Taf Fawr	Waterfall	160	992 202	204
27	Cwm Llwch	Nant Cwm Llwch	Waterfalls	160	SO 006 227	79
28	Ffrwdgrech	Nant Cwm Llwch	Waterfalls	160	021 264	81
29	Talgarth	Enig	Pwll y Wrach	161	172 327	85
30	Capel y Ffin	Nant y Bwch	Unmarked	148	236 328	205
31	Erwood	Bach Howey	Unmarked	148	108 428	206
32	Pant-y-Celyn	Cadney	Waterfalls	147	SN 894 551	206
33	New Radnor	Tributary of Summergil Brook	Water-break-its-Neck	148	SO 185 601	87
34	Marchnant	Marchnant	Waterfalls	147	SN 905 602	91
35	Rhiwnant	Nant Parad	Waterfall	147	892 608	91
36	Ciloerwynt	Claerwen	Waterfall	147	885 628	89
37	Garreg Ddu Reservoir	Unnamed	Waterfalls	147	897 641	91
38	Garreg Ddu Reservoir	Unnamed	Waterfall	147	914 660	91
39	Dderw	Tributary of Wye	Waterfalls	147	940 695	91
40	Claerwen Reservoir	Nant Hirin	Ffrwd Wen	147	846 705	89
41	Cwm Coch	Nant y Sarn	Waterfalls	147	934 713	91
42	St Harmon	Marcheint Fawr	Waterfall	136	959 730	207
43	Rhosgree	Tributary of Lugg	Waterfall	148	SO 183 736	208
44	Glynhafren	Tributary of Severn	Waterfall	136	SN 895 838	209
45	Hafren Forest	Severn	Unmarked	135	844 898	93
46	Staylittle	Trawsnant	Waterfall	136	912 930	209
47	Forge	Hengwm	Waterfall	135	744 934	95
48	Dylife	Twymyn	Ffrwd Fawr	135	874 941	97
49	Glasbwll	Llyfnant	Pistyll y Llyn	135	SN 754 942	99
50	Cwm y Rhaeadr	Llyfnant	Waterfalls	135	753 962	101
51	Llangadfan	Nant Ysguthan	Waterfalls	125	SH 947 125	210
52	Tycrwyn	Tributary of Alan	Pistyll y Craig Ddu	125	SJ 095 189	211
53	Lake Vyrnwy	Unnamed	Waterfalls	125	SH 994 206	211
54	Lake Vyrnwy	Eiddew	Waterfalls	125	953 246	211
55	Pennant Melangell	Goch	Pistyll Gyfyng	125	SJ 018 246	103
56	Pennant Melangell	Tanat	Waterfall	125	008 276	103
57	Llanrhaeadr-ym-Mochnant	Disgynfa	Pistyll Rhaeadr	125	073 296	105

	Near Place Name	*Name of Waterfall River*	*Waterfall as described on OS Map*	*OS Sheet No.*	*National Grid Ref. No.*	*Page*
	DYFED					
58	Llandybie	Loughor	Waterfall	159	SN 643 152	213
59	Brynamman	Nant Pedal	Waterfall	160	695 161	77
60	Rosebush	Syfni	Syfynwy Falls	145	062 291	213
61	Cenarth	Teifi	Unmarked	145	273 416	107
62	Cilycwm	Merchon	Waterfall	147	732 418	111
63	Cilycwm	Nant Rhosan	Waterfall	147	752 428	111
64	Cilycwm	Rhaeadr	Waterfall	147	755 437	111
65	Tresaith	Unnamed	Waterfall	145	280 517	213
66	Strata Florida	Mwyro	Waterfall	147	784 647	214
67	Tynygraig	Tributary of Ystwyth	Unmarked (Caradoc)	135	694 696	215
68	Dologau	Nant Gau	Waterfall	135	785 707	113
69	Dologau	Tributary of Ystwyth	Rhaeadr Peiran	135	772 738	115
70	Devil's Bridge	Mynach	Mynach Falls	135	742 722	117
71	Devil's Bridge	Rheidol	Gyfarllwyd Falls	135	743 775	119
72	Rheidol Falls Halt	Rheidol	Rheidol Falls	135	709 789	119
73	Rheidol Falls Halt	Nant Bwa-drain	Unmarked	135	714 789	119
74	Parson's Bridge	Tributary of Rheidol	Unmarked	135	749 789	119
75	Furnace	Einion	Unmarked	135	686 952	216
	CLWYD					
76	Llanarmon D.C.	Ceiriog	Waterfalls	125	SJ 131 367	121
77	Aled Isaf Reservoir	Aled	Rhaeadr y Bedd	116	SH 916 598	39
78	Diserth	Ffyddion	Unmarked	116	SJ 057 794	125
	GWYNEDD					
79	Dolgoch	Nant Dolgoch	Dolgoch Falls	135	SH 654 043	127
80	Minffordd	Nant Cader	Waterfalls	124	727 118	129
81	Fairbourne	Unnamed	Waterfall	124	625 124	216
82	Arthog	Arthog	Arthog Falls	124	648 145	133
83	Dinas Mawddy	Nant Craig Wen	Waterfalls	124	830 173	218
84	Llanymawddy	Pumryd	Pistyll Gwyn	124	884 196	135
85	Llanymawddy	Llaethnant	Waterfalls	124	897 215	219
86	Ganllwyd	Gamlan	Rhaeadr Ddu	124	720 245	137
87	Llanbedr	Cwmnantcol	Waterfall	124	608 267	219
88	Ganllwyd	Gain	Pistyll Cain	124	735 275	145
89	Ganllwyd	Mawddach	Rhaeadr Mawddach	124	735 276	141
90	Llanuwchllyn	Lliw	Waterfall	124	824 325	219
91	Llyn Arennig Fawr	Nant Hir	Pistyll Gwyn	124	843 366	222
92	Trawsfynydd	Prysor	Rhaeadr Ddu	124	667 387	147
93	Festiniog	Cynfal	Rhaeadr Cynfal	124	703 412	149

	Near Place Name	Name of Waterfall River	Waterfall as described on OS Map	OS Sheet No.	National Grid Ref. No.	Page
GWYNEDD (Continued)						
94	Pont yr Afon Gam	Cynfal	Rhaeadr-y-Cwm	124	SH 750 417	151
95	Rhyd-y-sarn	Goedol	Waterfall	124	686 427	153
96	Rhyd-y-sarn	Goedol	Waterfall	124	692 432	153
97	Pont ar Gonwy	Conwy	Waterfalls	124	782 446	161
98	Pont ar Gonwy	Conwy	Waterfall	116	808 453	161
99	Tanygrisiau	Unnamed	Waterfalls	115	682 455	155
100	Clynnog-fawr	Hen	Waterfall	115	414 478	222
101	Tyn-y-Cwm	Maesgwm	Waterfalls	115	730 492	223
102	Bethania	Cwm y Llan	Waterfalls	115	623 517	173
103	Blaenau Dolwyddelan	Diwaunedd	Waterfalls	115	694 517	223
104	Blanenau Dolwyddelan	Diwaunedd	Waterfall	115	692 522	223
105	Bethania	Merch	Waterfalls	115	634 522	177
106	Bethania	Merch	Waterfalls	115	634 525	177
107	Bettws-y-Coed	Machno	Machno Falls	116	808 533	224
108	Bettws-y-Coed	Conwy	Conwy Falls	116	809 535	159
109	Dolwyddelan	Ystumiau	Waterfalls	115	737 535	225
110	Bettws-y-Coed	Pont-y-Pair	Unmarked	115	791 567	171
111	Bettws-y-Coed	Tributary of Llugwy	Garth Falls	115	777 568	169
112	Pont Cyfyng	Llugwy	Unmarked	115	735 571	163
113	Bettws-y-Coed	Llugwy	Swallow Falls	115	765 577	165
114	Llyn Idwal	Unnamed	Unmarked	115	639 588	183
115	Llyn Idwal	Unnamed	Unmarked	115	644 589	183
116	Llanberis	Arddu	Waterfall	115	578 593	187
117	Llyn Ogwen	Ogwen	Rhaeadr Ogwen	115	648 605	181
118	Marchlyn Mawr Reservoir	Marchlyn Mawr	Waterfall	115	615 626	187
119	Tal-y-Bont	Dulyn	Waterfall	115	756 684	225
120	Aber	Rhaeadr Fach	Rhaeadr Bach	115	665 696	189
121	Aber	Rhaeadr Fawr	Rhaeadr Fawr	115	668 699	193

Glossary of Welsh Words

ab, ap	son of
aber	estuary
afon	river
allt	wooded slope, hillside
bach, f. fach	small, little
ban, pl. bannau	peak
banc	bank, hillock
barcut	kite
bedd	grave
bera	stack
blaen, pl. blaenau	head of valley
bont	(*see* pont)
braich	arm
brenin	king
brith, pl. brithion	speckled
bryn	hill
buarth	yard
bwa	arch
bwch	buck
bwlch	gap, pass
bwll	(*see* pwll)
bychan	smaller, lesser
cadair, cader	seat
cae	enclosure, field
caer	fort, stronghold
cam	crooked
capel	chapel
carn, carnedd	cairn, rock
carreg, pl. cerrig	stone
castell	castle
cau	hollow, enclosed
caws	cheese
cigfran	raven
cil	nook, retreat
clogwyn	cliff, crag
clun	meadow
coch	red
coed, pl. coedydd	wood
corn	horn
cog	cuckoo
crib, pl. cribau	crest
craig, pl. creigiau	rock
cras	arid
criafolen	rowan tree (mountain ash)
croes	cross
cwm	cwm, valley
cwn	dogs
cwar	quarry
cwrt	court
cyfyng	narrow
cymer, pl cymerau	confluence, junction
delyn	(*see* telyn)
dinas	fortress
diserth	retreat, wilderness
dol	dell, meadow
du, (f) ddu	black, dark
drws	door, gap
dwfn	deep
dwfr, dŵr	water
dyffryn	valley
dywarchen	(*see* tywarchen)
eglwys	church
einion	anvil
eira	snow
esgair	ridge
eryri	eyrie, eagle's nest
fan	(*see* ban)
fawr	(*see* mawr)
fechan	(*see* bychan)
felin	(*see* melin)
filiast	(*see* miliast)
ffin	boundary
ffordd	road, way
fforest	forest
ffrwd	stream, torrent
ffynnon	spring, well
gaer	(*see* caer)
gam	(*see* cam)
garn	(*see* carn)
garreg	(*see* carreg)
garth	enclosure, garden
glas	blue, green
glyn	glen, valley
goch	(*see* coch)
gog	(*see* cog)

golau	light
griafolen	(*see* criafolen)
gwennol	swallow
grisiau	stairs, staircase
gwaun	moorland
gwrach	witch
gwyn	white
hafod	summer dwelling
hen	old
hendre	winter dwelling
hir	long
hiraethus	longing
hirwaun	long meadow
hyll	ugly
isaf	lower, lowest
llaeth	milk
llan	church, parish
llech	slab, stone
lliw	colour, form
llugas	light
llwch	lake
llwyd	brown, grey
llwyn	bush, grove
llyn	lake
llygad	eye
maen	stone
maes	field, plain
march	stallion
mawr	great, big
melin	mill
mellt	lighting
merch	daughter, girl
mignen	bog, swamp
miliast	greyhound bitch
moel	bare hill
moch	pigs
morynion	maidens
mynach	monk
mynydd	moorland, mountain
nant	brook, stream
newydd	new
nos	night
oen	lamb
ogof	cave
pair	cauldron
pandy	fulling mill or pool
pannwr	fuller
parc	field, park
pedol	horseshoe
pen	top
penrhyn	cape, promontory
pentre	homestead, village
pistyll	spout, waterfall
plas	hall, mansion
pont	bridge
porth	gateway, harbour
pwll	pit, pool
rhaeadr	waterfall
rhiw	hill, slope
rhos	marsh, moor
rhyd	ford
saer	carpenter
saethau	arrows
sant, saint	saint
scŵd, sgŵd	cascade, cataract, waterfall
sych	dry
tal	tall
tâl	toll
tan	end, under
tap	tap
telyn	harp
tre, tref	homestead, hamlet
traws	direction
tri	three
twll	hole
tŵr, pl. tyrau	tower
twrch	boar
tŷ	house
tywarchen	turf
uchaf	upper
wen	(*see* gwyn)
wennol	(*see* gwennol)
wrach	(*see* gwrach)
wŷn	(*see* oen)
y, yr	of, of the
ych	ox
yn	in
ysbyty	hospice, hospital
ysgŵd	waterfall
ystrad	vale, valley floor
ysguthan	wood pigeon

Bibliography

Beach, M.H., *Fisheries Research Technical Report*, no 78 MAFF, 1984)
Borrow, George, *Wild Wales* (John Murrary, 1919)
Brecon Beacons National Park (HMSO, 1966)
British Regional Geology—South Wales (HMSO, 1975)
British Regional Geology—North Wales (HMSO, 1961)
Brycheiniog (Various), *Proceedings of the Brecknock Society*
Giraldus Cambrensis, *Itinerary, circa 1188* (translated by Sir Richard Colt Hoare, 1806)
Carr, H.R.C. & Lister, G.A., *The Mountains of Snowdonia* (Crosby Lockwood, 1948)
Condry, W.M., *The Snowdonia National Park* (New Naturalist Series, Collins, 1966)
Conran, A., *Penguin Book of Welsh Verse* (1967)
Cumberland, George *An attempt to describe Hafod* (London, printed by W. Wilson, 1796)
Davies, W.H., *Collected Poems* (Jonathan Cape, 1940)
Davies, Margaret (ed.), *Brecon Beacons National Park Guide* (1967)
Drayton, Michael, *Polyolbion* (1622)
Fearnsides, W.G., *The Geology of Arenig Fawr and Moel Llyfnant* (1905)
Grigson, Geoffrey, *Country Writings* (Century Publishing, 1984)
Hopkins, G.M., *Poems* (Oxford University Press, 1964)
Inglis-Jones, Elisabeth, *Peacocks in Paradise* (Faber, 1950)
Jenkins, Elis (ed.), *Neath and District* (1974)
Jones, J.R., *The Salmon* (Collins, 1959)
Mid Wales Investigations Report (HMSO, 1955)
North, F.J., Campbell, B., Scott, R. *Snowdonia. The National Park of North Wales* (Collins, 1949)
North, F.J., *The River Scenery at the Head of the Vale of Neath* (Nat. Museum of Wales, 1962)
Peacock, Thomas Love, *Philosophy of Melancholy* (1812)
Headlong Hall (1816)
Pennant, Thomas, *A Tour of Wales* (London, 1784)
Plomer, William (ed.), *Kilvert's Diary* (Jonathan Cape, 1935)
Priestley, J.B., *Thomas Love Peacock* (Macmillan, 1927)
Ruskin, John, *Modern Painters* (1843)
Shell Book of Wales (Michael Joseph, 1969)
Thomas, Dafydd, *Michael Faraday in Wales* (Gwasg Gee, 1974)
Trueman, A.E., *Geology and Scenery in England and Wales* (Penguin, 1971)
Vale, Edmund (ed.), *Snowdonia National Park Guide* (HMSO, 1973)
Vaughan, Henry, *The Metaphysical Poets* (Penguin, Book 1964)
Victim of the Beacons. The Story of Little Tommy Jones (BBNP/JAC, 1975)
Walks in Gwydyr Forest (Forestry Commission, 1971)
Watts Dunton, T., *Aylwin* (Oxford University Press, World's Classics, 1950)
Wordsworth, W., *Collected Poems*

Index

(All waterfalls are indexed alphabetically under 'Waterfalls')